PARASITE PARADISE

D1674712

A MANIFESTO FOR TEMPORARY ARCHITECTURE AND FLEXIBLE URBANISM

PARASITE PARADISE
A MANIFESTO FOR TEMPORARY ARCHITECTURE AND FLEXIBLE URBANISM

NAi Publishers / **SKOR**

This publication coincides with the
event 'Parasite Paradise' in Leidsche Rijn,
organized by Beyond-Leidsche Rijn.
www.beyondutrecht.nl

INTRODUCTION

Parasites – this word was uttered during one of the many preparatory discussions for 'Beyond', the multiple-year scenario for art in Leidsche Rijn, a government-designated 'Vinex' site for urban expansion near Utrecht. Peter Kuenzli, who chaired the task force entrusted with framing the scenario, had become taken with the ideas of the Parasite Foundation which propagated light forms of urbanism and architecture. P.A.R.A.S.I.T.E.S. is a near-acronym for 'Prototypes for Amphibious Readymade Advanced Smallscale Individual Temporary Ecological Houses', an umbrella term covering a wide range of small-scale exercises in art, architecture and urbanism that delivered a nimble-witted if serious commentary on the over-regulated real-estate practices of the day.

At the time when this subject took root in the arts plans for Leidsche Rijn and became part of the programme for the draft scenario 'Beyond – Leidsche Rijn', it seemed as though Europe was awash with expectations on the mobility front. Besides the activities of the Parasite Foundation, which were targeted principally at an architecturally oriented exhibition circuit, Dutch magazines on architecture and urbanism such as *Archis* and *de Architect* focused their gaze on this phenomenon. In 2000, *Quaderns*, their Catalan counterpart, published a special issue entitled *Flashes* about current ephemeral structures throughout the world, and still other magazines looked to historical examples by Buckminster Fuller, Archigram and others. In 2002 the Vitra Design Museum in Weil am Rhein mounted the exhibition 'Living in Motion', which dwelt at length on Fuller's *Dymaxion House* as well as on the portable homes of nomadic peoples. Remarkably, its focus was not restricted to the architectural field but also included projects by graphic designers and visual artists. And in 2001 the Dutch arts magazine *Metropolis M* devoted an issue to future dwelling, also in the digital sense.

Over the past few years a good many artists have created spaces for human physical presence and stimulated use of the spatial installations presented at exhibitions and festivals and

TOM VAN GESTEL

in the public realm. These not infrequently involved caravans and containers. In 2001 the Westfälisches Landesmuseum in Münster presented 'Plug In: Unity and Mobility', an exhibition that set out to explore travel, dwelling and communicating from a visual arts perspective. Nineteen artists took part including Joep van Lieshout, Tobias Rehberger, Carsten Höller, Christine and Irene Hohenbüchler and Dan Peterman.

And yet most of these exhibitions went no further than showing models and small-scale interventions that were illustrative of the phenomenon and little more. The keywords were mobility, deregulation, network society, freedom, speed and individualism.

Meanwhile SKOR, the Foundation for Art and Public Space, was approached by Marjolijn Boterenbrood of Stichting Werk Spoor, a laboratory of artists and scientists in areas of transformation. This last-named body had set itself the task of bringing to the attention of policy-makers and politicians the exceptional nature and historical significance of the Stork grounds in Amsterdam. This artificial island of more than three centuries' standing is one of the few remaining industrial complexes near the centre of Amsterdam and has been key to Amsterdam's economic welfare since the early days of the Dutch East India Company. Stichting Werk Spoor hoped to advance a more considered use and layout for the site, supported in its endeavour by the site's new owner (Heijmans IBC Vastgoedontwikkeling). A further objective besides the work of observing, recording and scanning carried out by artists, writers and scientists, was to be a spectacular public festival.

Originally SKOR acted mainly as an interlocutor and consultant. During one of the brainstorming sessions the owner expressed the wish to grant small lettable business units to a more footloose brand of user. The vibrancy on site would be well served by constantly fluctuating small-scale activity alongside the domiciles of a few major enterprises. At the same time, there arose the problem of the factory sheds that were either unoccupied or in need of restoring, along with as yet unallocated parts of the grounds. The same held for Leidsche Rijn, where undefined or as yet undeveloped areas of

H.OME. Frank Halmans

Tampa Skull. Atelier van Lieshout

Favela. Atelier van Lieshout

paraSITE. Attila Foundation

Futuro. Matti Suuronen

Snail Shell System. n55

Snail Shell System. n55

'Mobile Architecture for Stork', SKOR 2001.
Photo's Theo Krijgsman

land gave cause to discuss the possibility of including temporarily deployable or mobile structures in the programme of the arts project 'Beyond – Leidsche Rijn'. So began an unexpected relationship between the Vinex location of Leidsche Rijn and a historic industrial site in Amsterdam. The Stork grounds could act as a test area for mobile architecture and habitable art which could then be tried out at a later stage in Leidsche Rijn at a greater scale and in the reality of day-to-day life. It was decided to use the Stork grounds and five factory sheds (Van Gendthallen) to mount an exhibition of unique relocatable built structures so that the phenomenon could be experienced at 1:1. Additionally, Heijmans IBC, the Amsterdam Arts Foundation (Amsterdams Fonds voor de Kunst), Stichting Werk Spoor and SKOR joined forces in organizing a limited entry competition to develop mobile live-work units for artists. This was a way of gauging the wishes and capabilities of artists in developing something of this kind. At the same time it was a crafty attempt to put the regulations on land use plans to the test.

It was in the last weekend of September 2001 that Stichting Werk Spoor held an event whose title translates as 'Mobile Architecture for Stork', after a scenario by Dick Hauser. Actors in work clothes led visitors across the grounds, describing its history and drawing the mobile objects scattered about the site into their act. Beginning at Piet Hein Eek's garden shed doing duty as a ticket office, the public then made its way past Eva Hertzsch and Adam Page's *Executive Box* to Koers Zeinstra Van Gelderen's *Tuimelhuis*, admired the *Airstream Caravan* installed at a corner of the Van Gendthallen, found themselves in a *paraSITE* courtesy of Kas Oosterhuis, Menno Rubbens and Ilona Lénárd, were almost run over by Gert 28's *Carovan*, got a little uptight in N55's *Snail Shell System* before finally entering the Van Gendthallen where they could tarry a while in Joep van Lieshout's *Tampa Skull* and *Favela*, Dré Wapenaar's *Winterbivak* or Jack Brandsma's *Movable Furnishings*. Visitors gaped at Alicia Framis's *Billboardhouse* and Matti Suuronen's *Futuro*, which hosted discussions on the future of the Stork grounds, and quenched their thirst in Frank Halmans's *H₂OME*. A forklift truck chugged round on a ceremonial platform bearing the results of the design competition.

In the next few weekends until mid January 2002, the exhibition continued in a slightly different configuration plus Yuri Leiderman and Vadim Fishkin's *Hotelit*, without Dick Hauser's performance but with films and discussions instead.

Those invited by SKOR and the Amsterdam Arts Foundation to take part in the design competition were Henrik Plenge Jakobsen, Klaas Kloosterboer, Luc Deleu, Dirk van Lieshout, Phantombüro, Dominique Gonzales-Foerster, Liesbeth Bik and Jos van der Pol (Bik VanderPol) and André van Bergen. The last four were awarded a follow-up task. In the end, André van Bergen's design for a live-work unit was chosen for construction in the Stork grounds. His proposal consisted of a train of spaces that clipped onto an under-carriage of trailers. The other three worked-up designs were to be given sites of their own elsewhere, which on investigation eventually turned out to be Leidsche Rijn.

The exhibition created a great deal of interest, also among the press. It was decided to give the parasites component priority in the Leidsche Rijn art programme and then try it out elsewhere under the aegis of SKOR. One project where the subject was raised was that of the Southern Axis (Zuidas) in Amsterdam, thereby legitimating SKOR's generous support of the 'school parasites' designed by Barend Koolhaas, Alex van de Beld and Christoph Seyfert for the WIMBY! (Welcome into My Backyard!) project in the satellite town of Hoogvliet near Rotterdam.

Parasites, light urbanism, mobile architecture, transportable architecture – all are terms with different meanings and charges that are an open invitation for careless and imprecise use. The phenomenon is not new and has consciously or unconsciously broken surface with clockwork regularity over the last 100 years. The causes and motives are as diverse as the physical expressions. At times they have a deeper underlying social, economic or technological reason; often the phenomenon appeals to an instinctive yearning for freedom linked to a degree of comfort.

Never before has there been an attempt to relate unregulated desires for mobility to a suppressed human basic instinct. Is it as Constant Nieuwenhuys predicted as a member of the International Situationists in the 1960s, that technological ingenuity allows us to develop a collective lifestyle for liberated man, one based on play and mobility?

What is mobile architecture exactly? What is its significance for society and for the planning of architecture and urbanism as well as for the attendant legislation? What is the sense in mobile architecture, and the nonsense? What is the division of roles between art and architecture? This book is about all these issues. It is, hopefully, a document that places the 'Parasite Paradise' cultural event in Leidsche Rijn in an urban planning context, where not everything is fixed beforehand and changing needs can be flexibly met. It is also meant for all those other situations and places where the unbearable lightness of architecture is a real option.

THE ART OF UNSETTLI
MOBILE ARCHITECTU
SURPLUS VALUE

GIJS VAN OENEN

T he 20th century is no more, and the last remaining grass lots between motorways and railway tracks in the Netherlands have been designated 'Vinex' locations – target areas for new urban development planning. The small Dutch territory is now entirely caught in a matrix of land use plans, procedures and permits. Entirely? Well no, a handful of small unruly pockets of land are still stubbornly resisting colonization by the planning culture. It is round these indeterminate domains that my narrative unfolds. Stacked containers, dismantled masts; mobile architectures as undefined encampments, temporary refuges from the imperatives of public-private regulation. The question is: what is the potential surplus value of these artistic havens? How can they hold their own within PPP, the empire of Public Private Planning – that is to say, how can they survive without becoming permanently alienated from PPP society, while simultaneously resisting its assimilating tendencies? How can we voice the feeling that these final indigestible remains of Dutch soil are of vital importance for the political, cultural and social metabolism of a Netherlands otherwise planned to capacity?

This feeling – that mobile-architectural artworks enable counterpunching in times of PPP – is not without problems; the history of artistic intervention in political plan-making has always been a touchy business. Take the Italian poet Gabriele D'Annunzio who in 1919 set sail with a small band of adventurers to capture the town of Fiume (now Rijeka in Croatia), where he proclaimed a 'free state' that lasted a year or so (anyway, longer than the average postwar Italian government). Then there are artists who are not actually on a political mission, limiting themselves instead to producing politically engaged

14

AND ITS POLITICAL

art; right or left, these also appear somewhat suspect. Think of Leni Riefenstahl's film *Triumph des Willens* or Bertolt Brecht's *Lehrstücke* (learning plays). Of course more appealing examples also exist, such as the Social-Realist murals of Diego Rivera in Mexico, Picasso's *Guernica*, or *AVL-Ville*, the anarchistic free state founded by the Dutch artist Joep van Lieshout in Rotterdam's former docklands. It's a difficult genre – but not an impossible one.

The notion of 'free state' as wielded by Van Lieshout actually reflects very well both the strength and the problematic side of the mildly anarchistic order he aspired to in *AVL-Ville* (a free state that, like D'Annunzio's, lasted for about a year). On the one hand, this is a domain where normal laws and rules are momentarily suspended – a moderately transgressive zone where tinkering on is more important than measuring off, and improvisation takes precedence over permits. The accent in free state is on 'free': free from the bureaucratic propensity to intervene and regulate, from planners, allocators and inspectors. Once the Dutch weekly *Vrij Nederland* (Free Netherlands – what's in a name?) published an interview with an escapologist who for years had plied his trade in a travelling circus. He enjoyed his work, but preferred to let his wife deal with the red tape his self-employed business often ran into. 'I'd rather hang upside-down in handcuffs ten metres above the ground on a burning rope than have to discuss matters with a civil servant', he confided to the reporter.

That is the true spirit of the free state: a place without civil servants, where you are free to drop dead unsupervised – undisturbed, yes, but also uninsured and uncared for. Not everyone is cut out for this kind of freedom. But the free state has another obverse, which becomes apparent if we shift the accent to the second term: 'state'. Van Lieshout latched onto this as well, which is why he commissioned his own constitution and fitted a machine gun on a Mercedes pick-up truck, warlord style – deterring potential enemies all the way to the Heyplaat across the Maas river. The free state is a

15

state too, with its own rules, borders and means of enforcing order.

AVL-Ville was a state of its own that militated against what Van Liesfout was wont to describe as 'the state monopolies' – not just monopolies on violence but also on more mundane matters such as waste disposal, the provision of energy and sewerage. However, this political notion rests for many reasons on wishful thinking, reasons that are of interest to devisers of new humane game parks – or parasites. Firstly, political alliances, even regular nation-states like the Netherlands, have no further need of anti-aircraft guns. Unquestionably the Netherlands is a sovereign state, yet during the entire 20th century it has not been able or willing to seriously defy hostile forces In the War against Terror it dispatched ships in the direction of Afghanistan, but first made sure that 'no heightened risk' was to be expected (but then what is the point of going?), and sent fighter planes on condition that they wouldn't have to fight. 'Leaving church before the sermon', as the old Dutch expression goes. Cowardly? Maybe, but the valuable lesson here is that firepower is no longer a condition for sovereignty. Old-fashioned defence of national borders has been out of the question in our particular western dominions. These days Schiphol airport (and not the Rhine) is the main port of entry, or perhaps even more to the point: the service windows of social services departments, housing corporations, schools and hospitals.

This brings me to my second footnote to the political pretences of today's 'free states'. These days, institutions such as those named above are no longer just part of 'the state'. They have either become independent or gone commercial, having been commodified in the interests of efficiency operations, liberalization and a unified Europe. It is therefore no longer possible to engage in politics by taking over vital state organs, as one would have done in good old revolutionary times. Those organs have in fact already been taken over, that is to say, they have been outsourced and commodified in the name of PPP. These days, you can't simply proclaim an independent state; you have to 'repossess' it from a Kafkaesque network of public-private collaboration, driven by the liberalized eroticisms of deregulation and competition.

And that's a best case scenario. If we are not so lucky, we will be faced not with public-private collaboration but with their conflict instead. On the one hand we find an increasing proclivity for rules and regulations, by a government that is lured by the prospect of strict enforcement rather than toleration; on the other hand, we encounter a market system that seems to falter more than function. With the economy faltering and stock markets crashing, many dreams of public-private services go up in smoke.

How in these circumstances can we continue to project the contours of a free state within the tight building alignments and meticulously calibrated sight lines of the PPP-imbued Vinex areas? What are the parameters for practices of artistic freedom in the monocultural life of newly bred neighbourhoods? Well, these parameters can perhaps be found in 'parasites': unstable places, mobile fixations, nomadic nests, artists' impressions in the true sense of the word: no more – but equally no less – than 'impressions' that can be swept away over time, artistic markings acting as temporary stations for local facilities, from youth centre to local café, from billboard house to airstream caravan.

Here the 'state' in 'free state' refers less to public governance or national territorial borders than to a way of being, a condition or characteristic of living and dwelling in the new frontier of the polder. It is here that art must make use of what is locally available, what is vacant or disused, what has slipped through the cracks of the PPP matrix. In the absence of abandoned industrial heritage, such as we encounter in former dockland areas in cities such as Amsterdam, Rotterdam or London, it makes sense at locations like Leidsche Rijn to take those domains yet to be appropriated and have them temporarily function as free territory. We should take the word 'function' literally, as it is a less a question of establishing than of inciting, of having something happen, of setting the pace instead of pinning in place.

The aspect of incitement illustrates the fundamentally utopian nature of free states or independent territories. Unlike ideologies, which reflect dominant ideas and seek to enforce existing order, utopias are attempts to conjure up alternatives to the status quo. According to the sociologist Karl Mannheim, who introduced this distinction, a world without utopianism would be horrendous, a society of individuals only concerned with their own interests. He feared this would lead to a social science limited to techniques for adapting people, to a socialism that replaces the broad utopian perspective with the narrow-minded view of councils advising parliament and trade unions focused on mere details. Indeed, something resembling the political-administrative environment (*Umwelt*) in which we live today, and pretty much the reason why free territories – whether *AVL-Ville*, Leidsche Rijn or the anarchistic Free Radio 100 in Amsterdam – seek to achieve an autonomous state within a state.

Common to practical utopianism and mobile architecture is that they construct tangible, serious yet not top-heavy parameters/parasites for alternative habitats. In that sense, they are both light: like modern life generally they have moved beyond ideology, are fleeting, indicative and suggestive rather than normative or binding. This could be called conformist, and perhaps even opportunist. But on the other hand it means that the modern utopia does not feel the need to isolate itself from civil society and its emancipatory tendencies. Utopians are modern, emancipated citizens too – not least because the government (read the hypercomplex totality of public-private networks, or PPP) literally and metaphorically provokes it. Utopians apply for subsidies, engage in fund-raising, or work from a commercial basis the way Van Lieshout does. This is where 'state art' meets 'street art'; social recognition and artistic or philosophical pretence attain common ground and shared social objectives.

Apart from being light, utopian free states can be educational. This, again, derives from the nature of utopia as a direct, socially oriented way of life. A basic facet of utopian free territories is not so much the right to do as you please regardless of the welfare of others, as the experience that in the event of setbacks, problems or conflicts you have to look for a solution yourself without the support of priest, policeman or insurer. At times this leads to chaos, indifference and even disaster – see the recent 'free states' of Enschede (the fireworks explosions) and Volendam (the café fire). But there market ideology rather than utopia held sway. In less commerce-prone utopias, the ability to manage for oneself and with others takes precedence over filing claims, or settling up. This can only be done in a culture which in and through its very transgression of and relativism towards rules is able to develop self-regulating and self-restricting capacities. What our society needs above all is to restore, not clear-cut standards but the capacity to put up with deficient standards. And this for me is the essence of the much-discussed *gedogen* – 'tolerance practices', or 'forbearance' – in the Netherlands: not spineless or lax, but resilient and creative.

It is insufficiently recognized that an unruly legal order may well imply a strong sense of standards. Indeed, legal orders are well served by people who master the art of colonizing contumacious places, 'informal areas' and ambiguous zones in such a way that they do not turn illegal, chaotic or fundamentalist. It is exactly this colonizing that teaches one to develop ways of dealing with the wildness of daily life, ways that are more productive than the categorical rejection of unruly practices as illegal, or the commonplace rhetoric of 'the law's the law' and 'we'll just have to stick to the rules'.

This brings me to the legal-philosophical core of free territories and more generally of practices that are, shall we say, worthy of toleration, or forbearance – which to me is no disqualification but very much an honorary title. The point here is that illegal practices conducted within a legal order have a chance of success, that they get on speaking terms with that order though without immediately adopting the law's particular speech and accent. This, then, is the surplus value of 'mobile architecture light' in Vinex times: not occupying, retaining and prescribing but provoking, exploring and 'standing out' (*Ex-istenz*, in the Heideggerian sense). In an article in the contemporary arts magazine *Parachute* Patricia van Ulzen pinpoints a factor common to the work of both Rem Koolhaas and Atelier van Lieshout, that it performs 'according to the rules of efficiency and functionality and yet remains wide open for the bizarre and the intangible.' That for me is the most relevant parallel to be drawn between aesthetics and ethics, artists' workplace and political free state; creating and maintaining openness within the given order, advancing unruly order, learning to embrace wildness.

– Jennifer Allen, 'Up the Organization', in: *Artforum*, April 2001.
– Atelier van Lieshout, *The Good, the Bad + the Ugly* (Rotterdam 1998).
– Frank Manuel and Fritzie Manuel, *Utopian Thought in the Western World* (Harvard 1979).
– Gijs van Oenen, *Het surplus van illegaliteit* (Amsterdam 2002).
– Gijs van Oenen (ed.), *Ongeregelde orde* (Amsterdam 2002).
– Saskia Poldervaart, *Tegen conventioneel fatsoen en zekerheid* (Amsterdam 1993).
– Patricia van Ulzen, 'Atelier van Lieshout', in *Parachute*, 102, p. 44-56.

FROM CLUSTERS TO SM
FLEXIBLE AND TEMPOF
IN LEIDSCHE RIJN

S uburban districts are not blessed with a good reputation. In the past, sociologists like Riesman and Sennett have ruthlessly characterized the suburbs as the negation of the city's vitality and heterogeneity. Suburbs, they felt, were safe havens for middle-class families who had turned their backs on the chaotic and multifunctional city. All unknown and unpredictable conditions were minimalized in the suburbs. Suburban life had grown into a world-shunning sphere of personalized existence. The monofunctional suburbs lacked urbanity. And urbanity, after all, stood for mixes of function, for life's pressures and uncertainties.

This perspective is no longer true of the suburbs.[1] Population, lifestyles and behavioural patterns have all diversified. The residents of Leidsche Rijn come from the surrounding villages, older suburbs and the city of Utrecht. As villagers, suburbanites and urbanites they are still attached in some measure to their former places of abode. Their day-to-day life need not necessarily be enacted in the domestic domain. For an urban field of nodes, work areas and living environments has evolved at the scale of the Randstad. There are various centres for work, shopping, facilities, services, education and entertainment that residents can turn to. The suburban world is a mobile world; the growth of car use in Leidsche Rijn has exceeded all expectations. These days districts mesh in many ways with other parts of a larger polycentric urban field. An urbanity now obtains that no longer coincides with the compact city. What are the consequences of this 'network city' for local facilities, particularly temporary facilities?

At the start of the 1990s the American journalist Joel Garreau introduced the notion of 'Edge City' to describe the situation in which new centres were springing up in the urban peripheries that were ever more independent of the central city in their functioning and so not compatible with the classic suburbs where the only function was dwelling.[2] However, suburban developments on the facilities front are becoming dominated by processes of scaling-up. Outside the city centres, the Netherlands now has large-scale commercial facilities such as malls, multiplex cinemas and furniture and interior boulevards at places that are easy to get to. Another aspect besides commercial factors to play a role here is consumer behaviour. Their mobility enables residents to opt for facilities further from home. This behaviour does undermine any basis for facilities in their own area. We can see this scaling-up in public facilities too, from social services to educational institutes. Are we only on the threshold of a further scaling-up of public, retail and entertainment activities or should we expect a countermovement with more concern for small-scale facilities? In Leidsche Rijn, they chose scaling-up as the point of departure. The clusters of facilities are combinations of crèches, primary schools, amusement centres, sports halls, shops, offices and the like. Clustering various functions in a large building was claimed to be advantageous and save visitors time. This scaling-up does have advantages but also disadvantages.

The large scale is vulnerable, with greater distances enticing residents into their cars. It syphons off the few activities there are in residential areas. The large scale can rule out surprises, experiments and marginal economic activities. There is strict regimentation of the way space in and around buildings is used. And it plays hell with building delivery dates. In Leidsche Rijn the clustering of facilities means that shops are being launched much later than planned. The chorus of complaints about facilities failing to materialize is gathering force. Research has shown that in 2002 not one of the residents of Leidsche Rijn was satisfied with the range of shops then at their disposal.[3] Now that clustering has proved to be

IVAN NIO

21

an obstacle to flexibility in the retail on offer, there are calls to partly throw this principle overboard. This change of tack is a major stimulus for a reorientation within spatial planning, so that more attention is brought to bear on small-scale, flexible facilities.

Small-scale facilities would benefit the occupation strategy of Leidsche Rijn. In the 1990s Rem Koolhaas placed Bigness on the agenda; Irénée Scalbert is one who feels it is now time to reassess smallness.[4] Parasites can explore the meaning of this small scale, possibly as interventions offering flexible facilities. The advantage of injections like these is that there is something to do at different places in a suburb and that the genuine public realm there gains in both use and significance. In addition, small-scale facilities can nail a district onto the regional map. Small businesses can hold their own in the scaling-up process in terms of service, ambience or specialization. Examples include the baker whose top-quality pastries attract customers from far and wide, and a café whose ambience pulls in the crowds. In Amsterdam, the restaurant 'Kaap Kot' has brought early fame to IJburg, a settlement in the making east of Amsterdam. Other facilities such as a theatre, bowling alley and fitness centre can give a neighbourhood a cachet of its own. One of the tasks is to get the programme that has unfurled across the entire urban field back into the suburbs. It can give unique meaning to a place that reaches much further than that projected by a cluster of facilities dominated by ubiquitous Dutch supermarket chains like Albert Heijn and Blokker.

Bottom-up initiatives
In general, it seems that the residents of Leidsche Rijn are satisfied with their new house. But dwelling – feeling at home – involves more than the house alone. People are now making greater demands on their living environment. In this respect the planning profession has little notion of what 'being at home' means. Its design raises Leidsche Rijn above the average suburb. In addition, it focuses on incorporating archaeological finds on site and on planning clusters of facilities. But it has yet to become enough of a living tissue that it can

adapt and be appropriated by its residents. The story behind each Dutch suburb is still coloured by welfare state planning. The blueprints take little account of the spatial requirements of entrepreneurs and residents. Any future changes have to vie with fixed three-dimensional forms and fixed programmes. There is no room, it turns out, for all those entrepreneurs both established and new who have offered their services to Leidsche Rijn from miles around. In the 1990s Amsterdam district of Nieuw Sloten – itself hardly representative of an urban district – there are large corner premises along the thoroughfares where accountants, tax consultants and physiotherapists can set up shop. Why wasn't *that* used as a reference for Leidsche Rijn? In Spain, every new city block gets a ground-floor space for commerce and retail automatically. It is even bricked in beforehand to receive the expected private enterprise.

A new district benefits from a degree of excess, from space that as yet has no precisely defined infill. Such excess encourages enterprise and unexpected use. A justifiable criticism of Vinex sites is that they are sealed shut with an overfull housing programme, leaving little flexibility for unpredictable turns of events in the community. It's not just a shortage of facilities. Changes in population makeup mean changes in what people require. Adapting facilities to meet such changes invariably lags behind the demand. The problems vary from a shortage of places at a crèche and not being able to buy a takeaway to a lack of playing space. Those facilities that are realized turn out to be expensive and none too flexible. Spaces that are cheap and flexible to use are getting scarce in the Netherlands and nowhere more so than in suburban areas. New suburbs have no buildings of any great age and no cheap spaces able to accept a change of function. According to the Council for Housing, Spatial Planning and the Environment the dearth of suitable premises, especially cheap ones, is a stumbling block to innovation in suburban areas.[5] Additionally, the reserving of space for future developments is thoroughly at odds with the coercive land exploitation practices. The updated Leidsche Rijn Development Scenario recognizes the problem. The powers that be are now working towards an even spread of reservations through the districts, including accommodation for small businesses, cafés, restaurants, snack bars and saunas.

Instead of proceeding from a rigid definitive structure it would be better to look more in the region of an immanent spatial planning rooted in everyday life. Occupants should be in a better position to create their own social and physical space. Parasites can stimulate and accommodate spontaneous processes and undertakings from the bottom up. This is where parasites attack the institutionalized spatial planning, undermining prevailing concepts and launching ground-breaking proposals. These might be 'wild' facilities, say for parents with young children who want to set up a child day care centre, young people who want to meet others of their age, or residents who fancy laying out a tennis court.

The local aspect

Daily life in the suburb has largely become deterritorialized. Availed of various forms of transport and communication, residents are identifying less and less with their neighbourhood. This last-named does seem to be subject to reassessment, however. Tailbacks are getting to be more and more time-consuming. There is a growing desire among families and people who spend much of their time at home (for instance to work there) for local social networks and facilities. And children, the elderly and those of limited income have always felt a bond with the immediate surroundings. In a network society, the importance of the living environment could well increase, as being the only land shared by citizens who otherwise look to the world for their identity. And so we see a burgeoning concern for the local as a reaction to the space of flows – for a return to what the sociologist Manuel Castells calls the importance of place.[6] Which flexible facilities might increase the suburb's standing in the network city?

For many suburban households it is a difficult business attuning work, personal welfare and domestic chores. Two-income households with children are particularly mobile and it is they who suffer the most from problems of time and distance. Busy households need a well equipped residential setting with day-to-day facilities they can use with a minimum of time involved. The idea of clusters of facilities is intended to solve this problem. But the limited offer remains a stumbling block. The shopping centres provide no more than the prime necessities of life. For non-daily shopping residents are required to look further afield. Many suburban households use the car to stock up with the daily necessities for an entire week, and not always from the nearest shops. Having said that, it is a fact that

Pizzeria in Langerak quarter. Photo Ivan Nio

Mobile snack bar on the shore of Nieuwe Meer, Amsterdam.
Photo Ivan Nio

Drive-in beach with stalls selling chips and ice cream, Oostvoorne.
Photo Ivan Nio

Kaap Kot seaside restaurant, IJburg. Photo Hubert de Boer

residents are unhappy with having to leave the district every time they need a bicycle repair shop, toyshop, library or café. So local facilities could do with expanding beyond the day-to-day, although the limited number of customers is often a reason not to do so. If the standards are high enough, however, this lack of customer support is a restrictive illusion. Another solution is temporary facilities that flexibly pick up on changing resident needs. This can give street trading a boost. Leidsche Rijn already has a mobile pizzeria and snack bar. There are also a few market stalls selling fish, cheese, bread and flowers. It would be an interesting experiment to supplement these with a mobile cinema, takeaway, toyshop, specialist orthopaedic shop and cycle repair shop. These could trek from one neighbourhood or Vinex district to another in a caravan.

Temporary facilities can also stimulate one's mental rapport with a place. These might be facilities for the summer season – from a stall selling *poffertjes* (miniature pancakes) to a beach pavilion – or several times a year (fair, circus, travelling theatre). At least as important is that there is more space for festivities and communal rituals that briefly break up or confound the daily run of things. There are few suitable places for such happenings in Leidsche Rijn itself, though these are part and parcel of suburban life. At present the residents have to make do with cafés and clubhouses in the village centres of nearby Vleuten and De Meern. Disseminating the everyday even further afield can be done by bringing events like children's parties, weddings and jumble sales to the attention of passers-by.

For most residents the place where they live is not the principal domain for social contact. Suburbs are anonymous habitats. The 'extended school' clusters in Leidsche Rijn are designed as meeting places. In that respect they resemble the time-honoured 'neighbourhood idea' where facilities function as mainstays of the community. It is questionable however whether they will act as integrating frameworks. The fact is, the residents of a suburb divide into groups with differing tastes and preferences. Meetings are no longer conducted in the traditional sense but along parochialized lines between like-minded residents. Taking this into account, it is still possible to promote the emergence of social networks by so structuring meeting places in the district (sports clubs, community centres, schools, public spaces) that they really do work as places of encounter for whichever target group or lifestyle category responds to the offer. Again, specific facilities could be added to the clusters to generate a greater mix of, and exchange between, groups. Could parasites be able to stimulate further this capacity for exchange and encounter? And for which groups and activities? Will a temporary facility become a youth hangout or a place for the elderly to meet? Will it be used as a music practice room or as a trendy café for those in their thirties and forties? Every facility also encourages conflicts between groups. Between old and young, among young people and among adults of different lifestyle. Parasites can be the object of a symbolic struggle. Which 'tribes' will take over the units?

In conclusion

A suburb in the network city can have much to offer in residential terms but precious little else. It is the existing city and village centres that do the honours on the shopping, recreational and amusement fronts. This situation has given rise to a suburb with a split personality: a great place for dwelling, but for the rest you have to go elsewhere. Parasites can act as a mirror for planners and residents alike. Are the residents of suburbs self-appointed 'mobile network citizens'? Or are they forced to leave because the place where they live has almost nothing to offer them? This duality is made all the more oppressive by the simultaneous processes of scaling-up and scaling-down. The globalization and scaling-up of daily life has only increased the need among many residents for an eminently recognizable place of residence. Suburbanites are ambivalent when it comes to their own mobility. Though attached to it, they are at the same time looking for roots. Mobile units can reflect this nomadic way of life. As temporary facilities, on the other hand, parasites can also enhance a place's personality and habitability.

1 See also: A. Reijndorp et al., *Buitenwijk. Stedelijkheid op afstand*, Rotterdam 1998.
2 J. Garreau, *Edge City. Life on the New Frontier*, New York 1991.
3 O. Atzema, 'Problemen blijven. Bevolking en leefsituatie in Leidsche Rijn', in: *Leidsche Rijn Monitor*, 2002.
4 I. Scalbert, 'The City of Small Things', in: M. Stuhlmacher, R. Korteknie (eds), Stichting Parasite Foundation, *The City of Small Things*, M. Stuhlmacher, R. Korteknie (Red.), Rotterdam 2001.
5 VROM-raad, *Dagindeling geordend?* Advies 23, The Hague 2000.
6 M. Castells, *The Rise of the Network Society*, Oxford 1996.

IT'S NOT THE LAST WORD FIRST WORD OF THE NEX WITH PETER KUENZLI

*T*he Dutch planning profession, aided and abetted by the obstacles thrown in its way, leaves strips of unused land everywhere. Take the routes cleared for future motorways and railway tracks, where sometimes nothing happens for decades on end. It's a pity no-one does anything with them, as there are enough activities in need of cheap temporary space. These may have been pressurized out of the city, which is becoming less and less a source of new ideas. It makes you wonder why you couldn't cluster all those things together, or use that space for all kinds of temporary colonization and use – a bit free and anarchistic. I'm quite a fan of Bruce Chatwin, and in many of his books man ultimately is a nomad. Chatwin wonders whether it's in our make-up to spend our lives always in the same place. The parasites idea picks up on that. You carry your house with you on your back like a snail, in a manner of speaking. Everything is so spick and span in this country that there's almost no place for such ideas.

Peter Kuenzli was chairman of the task force that framed 'Beyond', the strategic arts plan for Leidsche Rijn of which 'Parasite Paradise' is one component. Once the plan was on the table, he turned his attention to other matters. For Kuenzli, along with his firm Gideon Consult, gets more pleasure out of setting processes in motion than bringing them to a conclusion. So, for example, he was director of the project office for Leidsche Rijn in the first phase of development, he saw the Rotterdam-Hoogvliet International Building Exhibition take off and is now supervising the reconstruction of Roombeek, the district of Enschede destroyed by the fireworks disaster of May 2000.

Kuenzli: *My firm doesn't live on government reports or fancy plans. We ensure things get done; we are into results that can be seen by those who are to make use of them. We get processes under way, seek out support and strong, firm contact. That's why I concentrate more on city life than on the city, more on the community than on the bricks. Once it's in motion, when I feel that the intention is safely in place, I move on.*

It was via the Hoogvliet exhibition that Kuenzli came into contact with the Parasite Foundation, a European network for parasitic enterprise set up by the Rotterdam architect Mechthild Stuhlmacher.

I helped her on occasion and was at the opening of an exhibition in Copenhagen where 40 models of parasites were showing. They were mesmerizing, I was converted on the spot. The plans were most inspiring as places to live or work. Since then I've been fascinated by the parasite idea.

I got into the notion of temporary spaces when we were gauging public interest in Utrecht for living and working accommodation, studios for example, on the outskirts of the city. Say in the zones where the A2 is to be extended and the railway doubled. They'll stay that way for at least another ten years, certainly in view of the state's current financial situation. We had no less than 300 responses – based on an annual rent of 45 euros a square metre, quite enough to be able to make something simple.

According to Kuenzli there are two domains where you already have something of a tradition of parasites: caravans and mobile homes, and houseboats.

But in both cases there's a tendency to pin them down instead of stimulating that dimension of freedom built into them. Houseboats these days are for the seriously rich; a residential mooring in IJburg must cost something between 450 and 500

OLOF KOEKEBAKKER

31

euros a square metre, with a fully equipped landing stage. Where does that leave you? I'd rather see a real houseboat, perhaps with a small tug to tow it to Friesland in the summer and back to Amsterdam for the winter. This also matches working patterns, which have become more mo-bile and flexible.

When I got taken up with the idea of parasites, I discovered that it appealed to a great many people. I admit it appeals to your romantic side, your unrealized wishes and needs. More and more people feel that living in this country is too confining. Almost every brochure you open at the estate agent's is of houses in a fast-track system of poured concrete. You can choose from ten different houses but they all look the same – and they all look like everything being built everywhere in the Netherlands. Only the names they get given are fancy – you can sense the underlying dissatisfaction in those names, the longing for some-thing a little more made to measure. The luxury they offer us is the luxury of inflated practical requirements and security regula-tions. A lot of us want something else: just basic spaces with a basic heater and if it's a bit colder in winter than in summer, fine. Where do you find such a simple house these days that you can do all sorts of things to yourself?

For the International Building Exhibition we looked round Hoog-vliet for zones and places with room for a parasites project. This turned out to be very many indeed: green zones doing nothing, buffer zones along the petrochemical industry at Pernis and the A15 – often fantastic spots, miniature paradises. If you were to place a sign there advertising land for rent for five years for a temporary house or studio, it would be snapped up in no time.

Kuenzli has also been looking elsewhere in Rotterdam for suit-able places for parasites in a joint stock-take with the City of Rotterdam's Urban Planning and Public Housing Agency (dS+V).

We found ourselves on quaysides where the ships used to moor five rows deep but that are now hardly ever used. We also dis-covered flat roofs often with a fair carrying capacity, certainly when they belonged to industrial buildings. A building like Las

32

Palmas can carry quite a load, in principle you could park a second building up there. Our dreams almost literally became reality in the parasite Mechthild Stuhlmacher set down on the roof of Las Palmas for Rotterdam's year as Cultural Capital of Europe. It is simply constructed using the German Dickholz ('thick timber') panel system which is at once structure, insulation and envelope, with basic ducting for electricity, water and waste disposal. A small construction firm was able to assemble it entirely out of prefabricated parts.

Do parasites require a special breed of designer?

Well, they certainly require a special attitude from their designers. What we're dealing with here is the idea of temporariness, mobility and reuse; and a parasite can only be moved if you can disassemble it. This is very close to what they call IFD buildings these days: industrial, flexible and demountable. It also shouldn't be high-tech but specifically low-tech and low-budget. For me an extreme but brilliant example is still the Swiss Pavilion designed by Peter Zumthor for Expo 2000 in Hanover. This was made entirely of wooden beams clamped together. When the event was over, off came the clamps and onto the back of a lorry went the beams to be used in some other future project. Designers could also turn to new materials, like Dickholz. I saw a design made by students from Helsinki who could manage the biggest load-bearing spans using ultra-light panels.

Autarkic thinking can produce some interesting ideas too. Parasites devised for extreme situations, such as the Scottish Highlands, sometimes include unusual solutions for generating energy. Composting your waste matter is the next step. And in the urban jungle a parasite obviously needs protecting. For example, you could make a container that can fully open up and seal shut.

Parasites are architecture and art at the same time. You're straddling the border. You might expect architects to approach it more in terms of fitness for purpose or the construction, and artists more in terms of metaphor and symbolism. But at the end of the day, I'm not that interested in whether a parasite is made or designed by an architect, an artist or a private individual.

'Beyond' is in the first instance an arts project. It's about creating scenarios for adding art as an extra layer, over a longer period of time, to the design for Leidsche Rijn. There was no mention of art in the masterplan and the development scenario. It's almost always like that: the art commissions are only handed out when the town or district is already inhabited and then you get endless public discussion on top of everything else. I wanted the art to be part of the colonizing process from the word go. For instance by making plots available to artists. By letting the artists know that those plots would be needed later for other uses, you're reversing the process: then it's the housing that follows the art, instead of the other way round. We invited intendants to commission artworks from them for the reserved plots. We additionally supplied the artists with archetypes of housing, such as a villa or a house with a through room. They had to take into account that the type allotted them needed to be placed within their artwork at a later date; nor could they reject this strategy on grounds of intellectual ownership. This way, the art has profound advantages for the district – a bonus that can perhaps be converted into cash since the land has become more valuable as a result.

With 'Beyond', and with the parasites that are part of it, Kuenzli is securing space for the unpredictable, the unexpected, in a new Vinex district like Leidsche Rijn.

Parasites increase the chance of something unexpected happening. The patronage is of another order, the financial structure is different and so are the requirements. This way, far fewer aspects are excluded in advance, providing that what is included isn't dangerous or offensive.

Many Vinex districts are crammed full to the last millimetre and most inflexibly too. This makes it almost impossible to mix functions, even though this and the aspect of surprise are at the very core of urbanity. This is why every unallocated hectare is a blessing. We in Leidsche Rijn are going to have to wait ages for those extra railway tracks, but once they are in place, the railway's intersection with the A2 will have a potential at least as big as that of Rotterdam-Alexander, maybe even as big as that of Amsterdam's Southern Axis. Only this is bound to take at least another 20 or 30 years. In the meantime you can better look for a parasitic infill than throw in three- or four-storey blocks of housing putting an end to any future development. This last example would also be a rash move economically, as it would insufficiently exploit the potential land revenues. That's how practical I am – I see parasites as more than just a cultural aspiration.

I'd say, let's just try it. We shouldn't want to know everything beforehand. You should resist the tendency to 'freeze' things when developing a new settlement. This was already part of the development scenario for Leidsche Rijn. You should realize that you are part of a much longer-lasting process of urbanization. It's not the last word you're adding, but the first word of the next stage. What we leave behind on site has to be capable of absorbing new things, rather than being the end of the line.

Futuro

Designed by the Finnish architect Matti Suuronen, the *Futuro* was developed between 1965 and spring 1968 by the firm of Polykem.[1] It is an elliptical orb made of 16 sandwich panels of glass fibre reinforced white polyester separated by polyurethane insulation. The orb sits on a steel ring resting on four legs. The *Futuro* has ellipsoidal windows and a door used in aircraft construction that drops down to become a stair. In name, material and appearance the *Futuro* is a perfect illustration of the optimistic space-age design of the 1960s.

The inducement to develop the *Futuro* came from a commission for a ski hut. Suuronen seized this opportunity to develop accommodation that would lend itself to mass production. The first example of what was then a nameless house (number 000) was ready in March 1968 and was used for many years as a ski hut. After endless peregrinations number 000 was bought by the Centraal Museum in Utrecht and transported there.

The house has a diameter of 8 m, a volume of 140 m^3 and a net floor area of 25 m^2. The interior consists of a vestibule with cupboard space, a compact bathroom with shower and toilet, a pantry, a recess containing a double bed, and eight chairs than can each be pulled out into a single bed. In the middle is a 'firebox' with a grill plate.

After number 000 came number 001, in bright yellow, which was given away to the Finnish television personality Matti Kuusla as a publicity stunt. This house was parked in Hirvensalmi in 1968.

It was only with number 002, made for the Finnfocus export fair in London in October 1968, that the name *Futuro* was thought up. In view of the attention the *Futuro* attracted there, Polykem decided to produce the house on a serial basis. In the years that followed, *Futuros* travelled all over the world from festival to trade fair. In the summer of 1970 an orange

Futuro made an appearance in Rotterdam at the C-70 'communication festival'.[2]

Fired by the success of the *Futuro*, Suuronen designed for Polykem a series of plastic buildings under the name *Casa Finlandia*, all designated with the letters CF followed by a number giving the floor area in square metres. According to Polykem the *CFs* could be used as a holiday house, a kiosk, a motel, a filling station, a car wash bay, a café and a bank branch, either as individual units or hitched together.

Despite the international esteem accorded them, neither the *Futuro* nor the *Casa Finlandia* became a commercial success. One major contributing factor was the tripling of the price of plastic after the oil crisis of 1973.

In the mid '70s, Polykem made an attempt to conquer the Soviet market. This elicited a large order from Sputnik, the young people's travel agency, and from Intourist which ordered a large number of *Futuros* and *CFs* for the 1980 Olympic Games in Moscow for use as holiday chalets, kiosks, cafés and accommodation for the competitors. The order was cancelled, however, when the Soviet Union lost a large part of the expected hard currency from the West after the USA, Japan and various Western European countries decided to boycott the Games in protest at the Soviet invasion of Afghanistan.

All in all, 20 *Futuros* were produced in Finland between 1968 and 1978 and at least 25 countries were sold a production license. Marko Home and Mika Taanila, who have made a film and a book about the *Futuro*, have managed to track down 30 worldwide, in Finland, Germany, Japan, the United States, Australia, New Zealand and the Netherlands.

1 This description is based on Marko Home and Mika Taanila, *Futuro. Tomorrow's House from Yesterday*, Helsinki 2002.
2 Peter de Winter, *Ahoy, E55, Floriade, C70. Evenementen in Rotterdam*, Rotterdam 1988, pp. 118-119.

photo's John Zimmerman, Fins Architectuurmuseum, Helsinki, unless stated otherwise

FUTURO / MATTI SUURONEN / 1965 – 1968

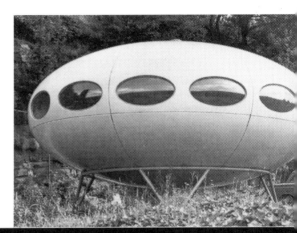

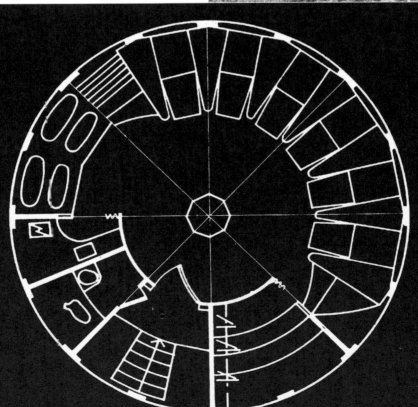

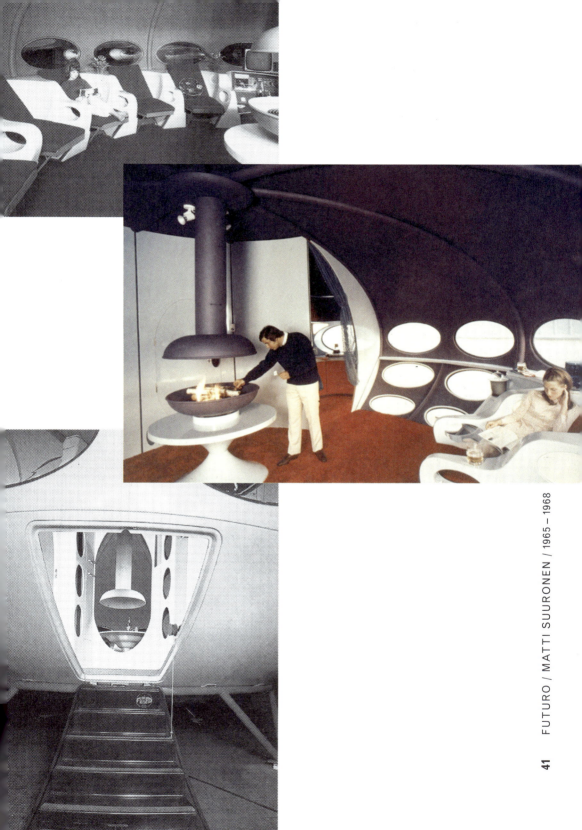

Hotelit

Hotelit is a combination of a hotel and an exhibition gallery. Visitors can stay there as if at a regular hotel and at the same time enjoy the art on display.

Wrapped in a grey steel envelope punctured with a regular pattern of glass panes, the container evokes associations with the functionalist hotel buildings of the 1960s. This association is enhanced at night when the windows are lit up. The interior has a plasterboard cladding.

The actual hotel room takes up almost the entire container, with only a bathroom next to the front door at one of the short ends. It is frugally furnished with just a bed plus telephone and TV. The walls and much of the floor are able to accommodate artworks. The opposite end to the entrance is entirely of glass so that *Hotelit* can also function as a public space. When the container is empty or when the hotel guest decides to pull back the curtain, the room can be viewed by the public. However, the guest can also decide to shut the curtain to create a private space.

The aim is to create a chain of such hotels worldwide. Until now, though, only one type has been built. This could be seen at the 'Waterproof' art event in Fort Asperen in the summer of 2001 and later that year in Amsterdam at the exhibition 'Mobile Architecture for Stork'.

At that time *Hotelit* was hosting the display 'Geologists at Sunset' and in Fort Asperen it was used as a hotel during the weekends. Ideally, its devisers would like to organize exhibitions every year presenting work varying from paintings to interactive multi-media installations and from objects to film, video, electronic media and programmes of specially composed music.

Hotelit's form – a sea container measuring 9.5 x 3.4 x 3 m including its envelope – is such that it can be easily transported despite its weight: the eight-tonne colossus is lifted in its entirety onto a trailer by lorry-mounted crane.

The Russian-born artist duo Fishkin and Leiderman developed *Hotelit* as a refuge for artistic individuality and for contemplation. They see present-day culture advancing in the direction of the superficial. They call it 'equalized communication', 'communication for communication's sake', 'communication on nothing' and 'communication on everyday life'. Individual opinion is on the way out, with the slow deep gaze ceding to superficial 'actuality'. The place of art and artists has become increasingly vulnerable and needs to be defended. In that sense *Hotelit* is the 'mental property' of artists and guests alike. You can spend the night inside art, so to speak, an internal situation. At the same time *Hotelit* is a sculpture in public space, an external situation. In other words, it is placed in space but floats in time.

authors: Vadim Fishkin, Yuri Leiderman
architects: Eugeni Asse, Vadim Fishkin
producer: DUM Association
made by: TRIMO d.d.((Slovenia)
sponsors: TRIMO d.d. (Slovenia)
Arcadia Lightwear (Slovenia)
Pristop Communications (Slovenia)
Mr. Sreco Kirn
with the support of: Fort Asperen Foundation,
Ministry of Culture of the Republic of Slovenia
Special thanks to: Tom van Gestel

photo's Vadim Fishkin

HOTELIT / VADIM FISHKIN, YURI LEIDERMAN / 2001

HOTELIT / VADIM FISHKIN, YURI LEIDERMAN / 2001

bed

window

2989

9125

Mobile Linear City

Mobile Linear City is a 'city' in storage.[1] It comprises six housing units telescoped together into a semi-trailer and hauled by a tractor. The whole then looks like a conventional lorry. Once parked, the city can be pulled out to its full length. Clad in corrugated sheet, each house has panels of different sizes that fold down from the wall into a table and bench, a bed and a rack. Separating the housing units are walls that may either be reflecting or translucent. Light enters through the steel grid floors. The last and smallest unit does duty as a community service centre and contains toilets, showers, a stove and a fridge.

This city is public; spectators can walk under the houses and look up through the floor unless occupants hide their homes with carpeting.

The bare, deliberately cold quality of this 'city', with not the slightest sense of intimacy, expresses Acconci's ideas about public space. For him, public space is 'space on the run', space that is slipping away from life. Here there is no place, and no need, for personal contact. In the age of viruses, the body has a shell to shield it from information and disease. Like a snail it carries its own house everywhere to protect itself. It visits places but never remains there.

1 This text is adapted from *De Rode Poort*, ex. cat. Municipal Museum of Contemporary Art (SMAK), Ghent, 1996–1997.

MOBILE LINEAR CITY | VITO ACCONCI / 1991

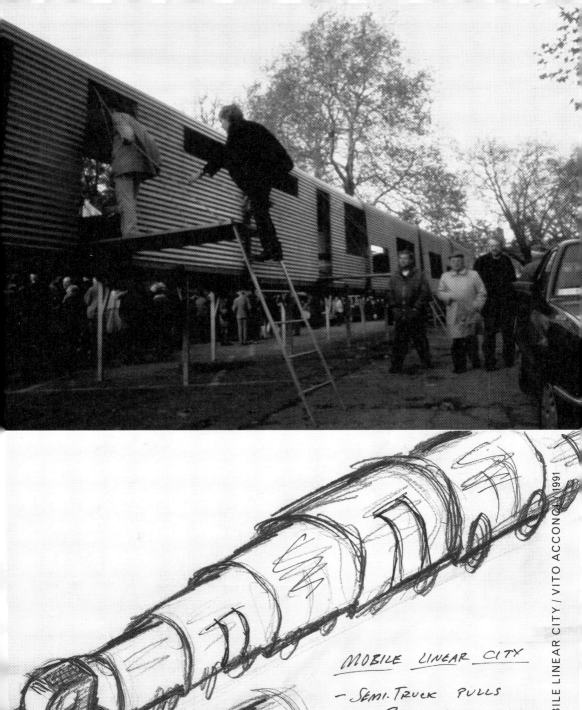

MOBILE LINEAR CITY

- SEMI-TRUCK PULLS
  BARREL-VAULT STORA___

- CITY PULLS OUT OF
  BARREL-VAULT

- EACH 'HOUSE' IS MIRRORED:
  BLENDS WITH OUTSIDE, PULLS
  IN OUTSIDE

- PARK SEMI; DRIVE TRUCK — DR___

MOBILE LINEAR CITY / VITO ACCONCI / 1991

Markies

Markies is a fold-out holiday house with the comforts of a regular house and, when folded up, as mobile as a caravan. Eduard Böhtlingk crafted this mobile home for the design competition 'Tijdelijk Wonen' (Temporary Homes), held in 1985 and organized by the De Fantasie committee in Almere. The prizes consisted of plots of land where the winners could put their ideas into practice aided by sponsors and subsidies. This ultimately produced the mini-district De Realiteit ('Reality'). *Markies*, designed on the principle that 'temporary homes are mobile homes', was one of those 17 winners.

When folded up, *Markies* has a surface area of 2.2 x 4.4 m, with all amenities for the modern-day camping enthusiast: fold-away furniture, a fridge, a cooker, a toilet and shower facilities. It is highly mobile too: in terms of weight and size, *Markies* meets the requirements for travelling on B roads. Once at its destination, the two sides are folded out with a simple press of a button into a true holiday house. The total floor area then measures 4.4 x 6.6 m.

The folded-out parts are oversailed by a pair of canopies (*markies* is Dutch for canopy). A dark orange canvas canopy covers the sleeping quarters. A fan-shaped partition divides the sleeping area of four beds into a children's and a parents' section.

The second canopy does duty as a roof for the living quarters and is sheathed in transparent PVC. This canopy can be opened up in fine weather to present a luxurious sun terrace. The sunscreen then provides a little extra shade as well.

The central body of *Markies* is made of sandwich panels 30 millimetres thick with a polyester top coat. A steel edge profile lends stiffness to the folding floor and is so shaped as to double as a gutter. A hinge specially developed for the project ensures that the canopies sit flush with the floor. Floor, canopy and sunscreen can be set in motion individually by means of three electric tubular motors.

The construction of the interior draws on poplar plywood finished with vinyl, synthetic resin or stainless steel.

The interior can be variously subdivided. In this prototype the arrangement consists of a fold-out bench, bed, chair and dining table. A tray can be folded out from the bench to put one's glass on.

Markies comes with a propane gas heater to provide hot water plus the option of a warm air convector which can be built into the smart ceiling of the core.

In 1996 Eduard Böhtlingk received the public choice award of Designprijs Rotterdam for the design of *Markies*. Since May 2002 *Markies* has been part of the travelling Vitra exhibition 'Living in Motion'.

photo's Roos Aldershoff

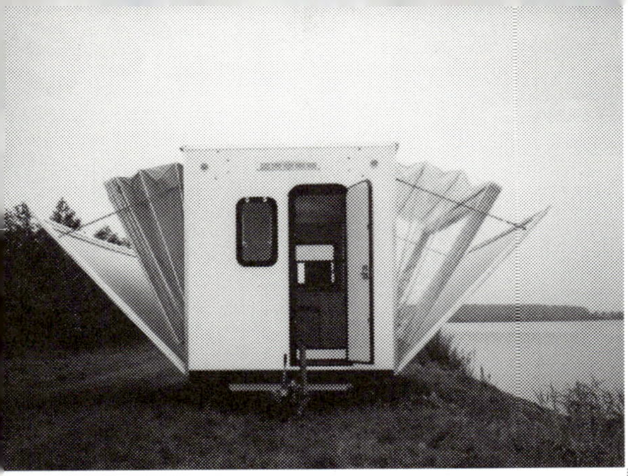

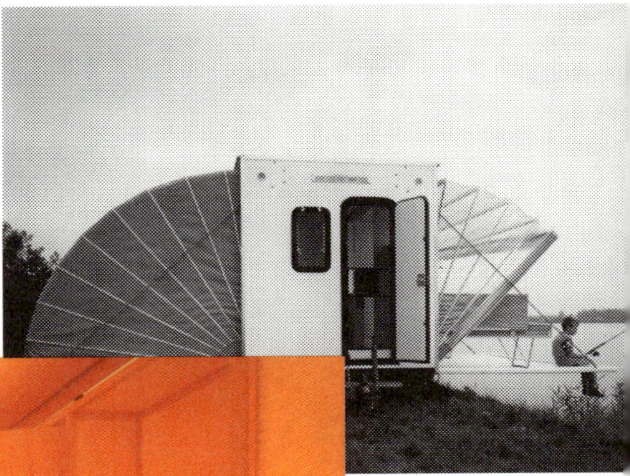

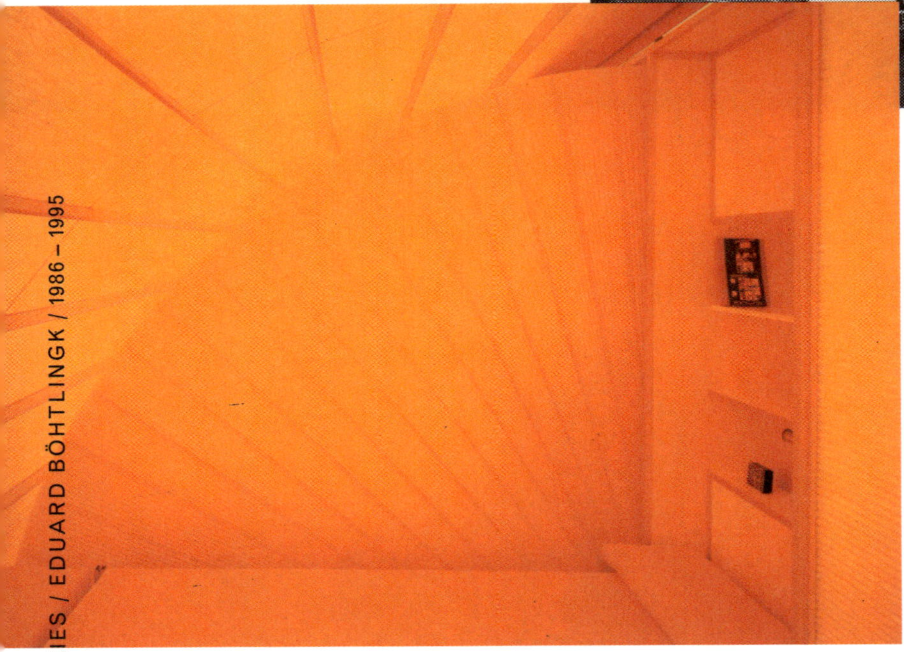

MARKIES / EDUARD BÖHTLINGK / 1986 – 1995

Pioniersset

This *Pioniersset (*pioneers' set*)* is a mobile farm consisting of a stable, a chicken run, a hay box, pigsties,
rabbit hutches, assorted machinery and fencing. All
parts are detachable and can be transported in the
container provided. This is simply placed on the trailer of a lorry and unloaded on site using a crane. The
Pioniersset can be parked anywhere and leads a self-
supporting existence. Its materials are made to last
and unscrupulously chosen for fitness of purpose. For
example, the door and window furniture looks ungainly
but extremely solid. Farm and stable have an external
cladding of corrugated sheet, with untreated wood as
the inner face. The rabbit hutches have an external
finish of black tar. Besides function and solidity one
can detect a whiff of nostalgia in the design, which
seems to reflect an almost romantic yearning for
nature. The two aspects combine in the *Pioniersset* to
produce one of the milestones in the work of Atelier
van Lieshout.

PIONIERSSET / ATELIER VAN LIESHOUT / 2000

Mini Capsule Side Entrance (6 units)

Mini Capsule Side Entrance (6 units) can be con-strued as a farm for people. The whole looks like a large polyester rabbit hutch, inviting comparison with the rabbit hutch of the *Pioniersset*. It consists of six tiny hotel rooms each able to house two people. The timber structure is clad in glass-reinforced polyester, giving a colourful, watertight and maintenance-free finish. The rooms are not much bigger than a double bed and are simply furnished with a mattress, bed linen, night light, clothes hooks, a power point and a bookshelf. *Mini Capsule Side Entrance (6 units)* is de-signed to function as an unmanned budget hotel.

MINI CAPSULE SIDE ENTRANCE (6 UNITS) / ATELIER VAN LIESHOUT / 2002

MINI CAPSULE SIDE ENTRANCE (6 UNITS) / ATELIER VAN LIESHOUT / 2002

Boerenwereldkeukenrestaurant

For the event whose title translates as '2003 – Year of the Farm' Marc Maurer and Nicole Maurer designed the *Boerenwereldkeukenrestaurant*, a mobile eating house (literally a 'farmers-world-cuisine-restaurant') which has been making a tour of all the provinces of the Netherlands. Every weekend it opens its 'doors' at another farmstead.

The restaurant can seat 100. Everyone sits together at one huge oak table which can double as a catwalk. The benches are extremely deep, so that you can also lie on them. The restaurant personnel have to walk across the benches and table to serve the food, encouraging an informal atmosphere.

The restaurant's design matches the ruggedness and simplicity of farm life with the sleekness and fitness for purpose of modern city architecture. This combination can also be read in the timber detailing which unites poplar (once the wood sort of the poor and of many in the farming community) and oak (once that of the well-to-do).

There is an unhampered view to all sides. The restaurant, which always opens whatever the weather, is heated and has its own lighting. In the event of a real downpour, a built-in tarpaulin is rolled out from the sides, bringing with it an air of intimacy and limiting views out.

© Johannes Abeling

Bar Raketa

It was their fascination with American follies – road-side restaurants in absurd shapes such as hotdogs, shoes or ice cream cones – that set the artists Inge Roseboom and Mark Weemen on the trail of *Bar Raketa*. Often with this typically American phenomenon of utilitarian architecture, the shape tells you what's inside: enter the gigantic doughnut and to be sure you can buy doughnuts in there. Not uncommonly however such buildings also propagate an idea. The old boot with windows in it has to get across the snugness of Mother Goose and the Indian wigwam stands for the adventures of the Wild West.

Bar Raketa is as much utilitarian architecture as it is an installation. Its form refers to the time when cosmonauts and astronauts vied for supremacy in space and it looked as though the cosmonauts were winning. That proud moment in Soviet history is given shape in a nifty space vehicle, its sculptural form a monument in terrestrial public space. But it's a monument with a false front. On entering the rocket you see not high-tech equipment but a Formica-top bar with drinking space for two. Gherkins are on offer from the display chiller on the bar and the walls are hung with snapshots and portraits. The photographs allude to the two Russian ladies behind the bar who seem to be running it.

Bar Raketa encourages a wealth of associations, something the artists deliberately invite. The bar can be disassembled at any moment and reassembled elsewhere and so has much in common with a circus act. Or is the sculpture merely a stage for the performance put on by the two Russian ladies? The photographs in the rocket seem as intimate as family snapshots in a living room, encouraging one to speculate on the ladies' past history; but visitors may just as easily think back on the small bars all over Moscow where tumblers of vodka are consumed.

By continually moving *Bar Raketa* from site to site Roseboom and Weemen stress on each new occasion another aspect of the interpretations it has to offer. It figured most heavily as a sculpture when featured in an art route, while at the Crossing Border Festival its theatrical and functional facets came to the fore. But *Bar Raketa* is before anything else an installation – a three-dimensional experience, whether from inside or outside, that seeks to tantalize all the senses.

The rocket consists of a steel structure with wooden trusses, the whole wrapped in a sheath of Bisonyl, a heavy duty fabric used for lorry tarpaulins. Its nose-cone can be opened using an internal mechanism. Standing on three fins, the rocket is eight metres tall with a maximum section of 2.7 m. It is fully demountable and is carried from site to site in a bus. For transportation overseas, the whole fits into a 20-foot sea container.

photo's Mark Weemen

BAR RAKETA / INGE ROSEBOOM, MARK WEEMEN / 2001

BAR RAKETA / INGE ROSEBOOM, MARK WEEMEN / 2001

Zusatzraum 1

Zusatzraum 1 – literally 'extra room' – is a prefabricated mini-house developed as an extension to an existing house or office. Transportable by lorry, it can function as a single unit attached to a house in the garden (homeworking office), as one or more units parked in a large hall (cellular offices) or as a free-standing office in public open space (office satellite). The entire structure is held aloft on three tubular piles six metres long. A crane lifts it onto this foundation, whereupon the whole is secured. The timber planks for the terraces are attached on site.

Zusatzraum 1 measures 4 x 2 x 3.5 m and has a working surface of 12 m^2. It divides into three volumes: a work space, a hall and a relaxation space above. There is room on either side for a simple terrace. The dimensions have been so chosen that *Zusatzraum 1* can be parked without the need for a building license. It derives its stability from the two supporting timber walls at the short ends and from steel sections set lengthwise and framing transparent red panels of plexiglass. Inside, the floors, walls and ceilings are clad with a hickory veneer in which all electrical plant is integrated. A fold-away drop leaf table and a row of book shelves the same colour can be drawn out from the wall. The room is lit by built-in programmable neon tubes which are able to evoke different ambiences; at night they can transform *Zusatzraum 1* into a luminous red object.

A prototype of *Zusatzraum 1* went on show in 2000 in Cologne during the Forum for Contemporary Architecture in Europe where it was used by Exilhäuser as a makeshift office. After that, its duties included acting as an extension to Exilhäuser's own office and as a mobile studio during the events organized by Kunstprojekte_Riem in Munich in 2001.

Founded in 1998, Exilhäuser Architekten owes its name, which literally means 'exile house architects', to the fact that its office is domiciled in the country-side in the vicinity of Munich, so the team has to travel daily from the city to the country.

© Edward Beierle

©Thilo Härdtlein

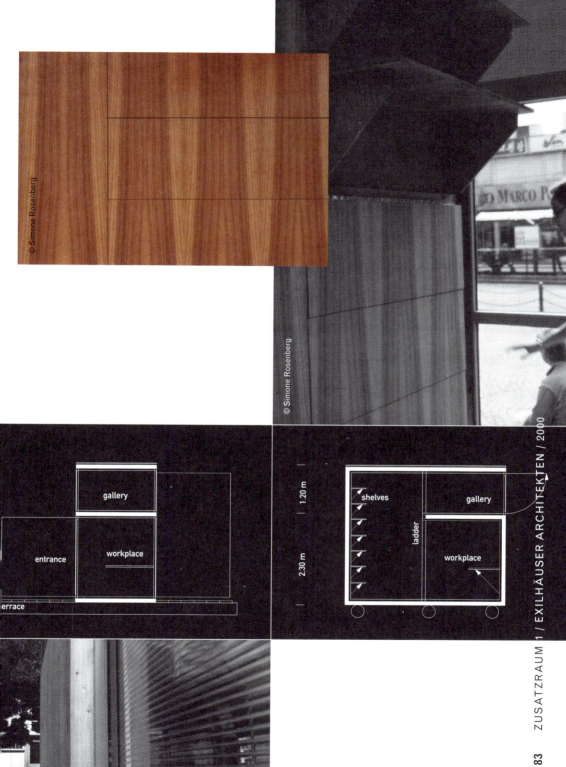

© Simone Rosenberg

© Simone Rosenberg

gallery

entrance

workplace

terrace

2.30 m   1.20 m

shelves

ladder

gallery

workplace

Zusatzraum 2

In 2002 *Zusatzraum 2* was tailored to the locality and scale of Enghien les Bains, a spa centre just north of Paris, for the fourth 'Biennale d'Art Contemporain' to be held there. On this occasion it was less a house or office, as in the original design, than a space for public use. This version of *Zusatzraum* consists of two units with a balcony on the first floor and a terrace below. It served as a meeting place and information centre as well as a platform looking out across the town and the water.

Orbino

In 1988 Luc Deleu made a sketch for *Orbino*, a mobile observation tower assembled from existing sea containers. Nothing more was done with this sketch until 2002 when the Noord-Holland Association of Art and Culture commissioned him to set up *Orbino* as a temporary exhibition gallery at the Nauerna waste disposal site.

Orbino is one in a series of container installations which Deleu has been assembling in Europe since 1983. All take the shape of archetypes (gateways, triumphal arches, bridges, arches and obelisks) and express temporality, mobility and mortality. The Belgian art critic Luk Lambrecht described *Orbino* as 'a monument and a playful nod to the invisible international trade by container; at the same time the work bobs between art and architecture.'

This approach derives from Deleu's propagation of the mobile medium of architecture as a possible response to housing problems; and from his call for 'Orbanism', a metaphysical and material principle for ordering the world using a dynamic balance between order and chaos and between individual and common property.

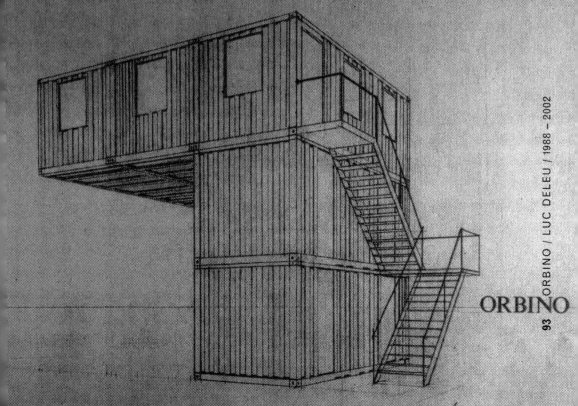

ORBINO

ORBINO / LUC DELEU / 1988 – 2002

paraSITE

paraSITE is an inflatable intelligent sculpture. Measuring 4.5 m tall, 6 m wide and 21 m deep, it can be set down anywhere. It made its debut in Rotterdam during the 'R96' media event; after that it went on a tour of the cities of Helsinki, Dunaújváros and Graz.

The interior of *paraSITE* is conceived as a web lounge with computers logged into the Internet. *paraSITE* is a sculpture with real-time behaviour. Every half hour it lights up brightly in a slow-motion flash accompanied by the dramatic sound of a crack in deep space.

For visitors who take their place at the computer, *paraSITE* mumbles its own *paraSITE* language developed by composers and artists at the different European locations. It's not immediately clear what *paraSITE* is talking about, but it is clear that we are experiencing another culture.

During its stay in the four European cities *paraSITE* was used as a field laboratory for local architects, artists and composers. These transformed the data that *paraSITE* sucks up through the net. Local data makes a particularly good meal for *paraSITE*! The composers developed a *paraSITE* language, something between words and music, by programming, sampling and transforming the data. Each city has contributed its own flavour to the development of the *paraSITE* language. *paraSITE* became more and more intelligent, and more and more beautiful as well. After a year, *paraSITE* returned to its breeding ground in Rotterdam.

Visitors can enter the silver tent through a narrow slit, man one of the computers and explore virtual space while being held in real time by light and sound.

Attila Foundation: Kas Oosterhuis, Menno Rubbens, Ilona Lénárd.
Sound, Language: Attila Foundation with Richard Tolenaar and Johan van Kreij.

95

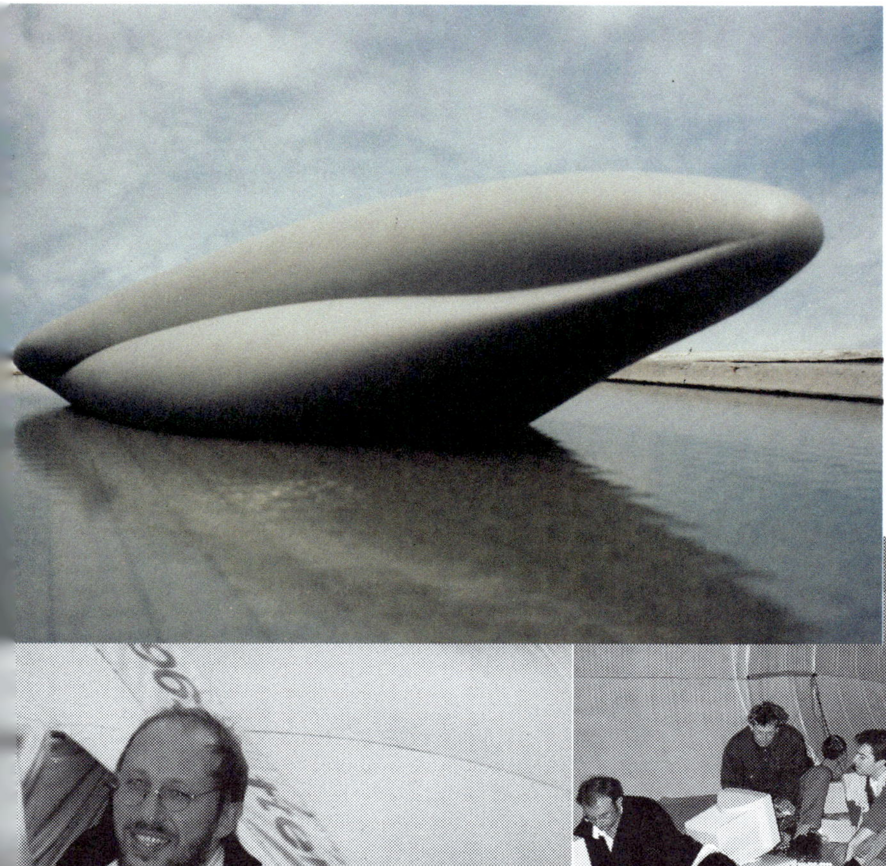

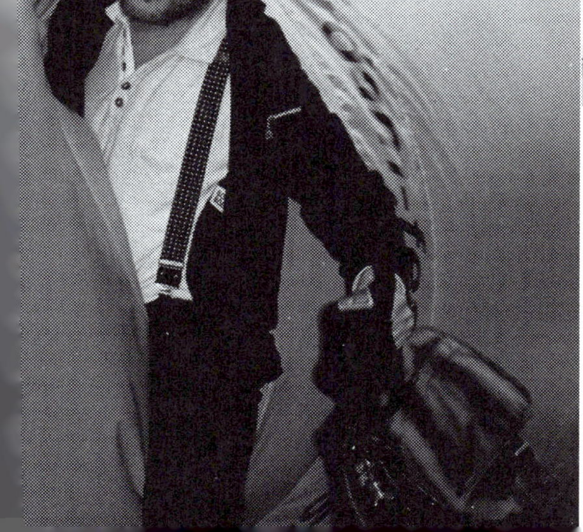

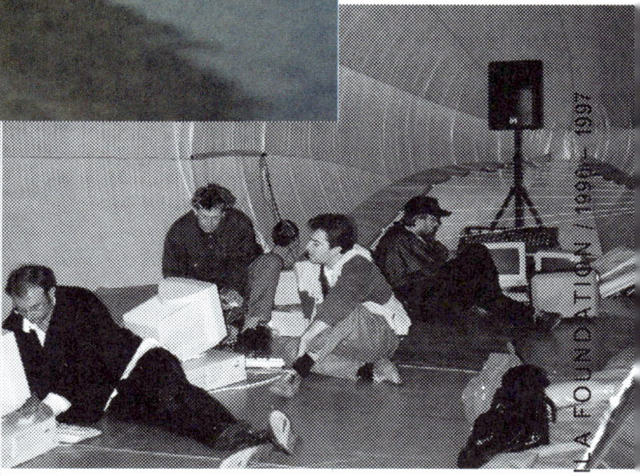

Billboardhouses

The *Billboardhouses* constitute a series of proposals for new ways of living (and living together) in cities today. For although social habits, forms of society and social structures are constantly changing, the basic floor plan of a house has remained more or less the same.

Alicia Framis is looking for new possibilities, as much for the floor plan itself as for ways of financing it.

The *Billboardhouses* are cubes entirely erected from billboards. Inside, the cubes are divided into a hard and a soft part. This is not the traditional domestic subdivision into kitchen, bathroom, living and bedroom because, although the norm for centuries on end, it is not suited to life as it is lived today. When all's said and done, a house is not a container for domestic activities but a place where the human body can achieve repose; soft and pleasurable and at the same time affording protection against the weather and against violence.

Framis hit upon the idea of a *Billboardhouse* in 1999 during a three-month stint working in Tokyo, where the houses are so small that domestic activities are enacted outside the home. Eating, washing, receiving friends, watching television and bathing are all done downtown. This relieves wives of their traditional domestic duties. The house itself is reduced to a place for relaxation and for storing personal belongings.

These *Billboardhouses* cost their occupants nothing. Companies pay for the houses' construction by advertising on the billboards. They are not just intended for the poor and homeless but for everyone living the modern life, at last freeing us from the house as a machine of subjection and family obligations; it allows us to transform the city into so many appropriated domestic places.

Only the *BillboardThailandhouse* has been realized until now. It was built for 'The Land', one of Rirkrit

101

Tiravanija's Thailand projects, and is tailored to that country's warm and humid climate. A wooden structure, it consists of three billboards on four tall poles to keep out rain and wild animals; the fourth side is open. The 'soft' centre of the house is screened off with a curtain.

The design for the *BillboardLeidscherijnhouse* (and a design it will remain for the present) consists of two identical houses for a couple who wish to live together but not all the time. Call it a house for weekend relationships. Measuring 4 x 2.5 x 2.6 m and raised on poles 2 m tall, it sports iron sections and transparent billboards. The houses can be telescoped together matchbox-style or pulled apart for privacy's sake. These 'well-matched houses', each consisting primarily of two billboards forming the long sides, can be slid together using a simple iron device on one of the short sides resembling a drawer that can be operated by one person. Various components of the interior can be hitched together for shared use and separated when the houses are uncoupled again.

The *BillboardThailandhouse* (2000) was realized for 'The Land', a project by Rirkrit Tiravanija (architect: Paz Martin, sponsors: City of Borken and SMAK, Ghent).

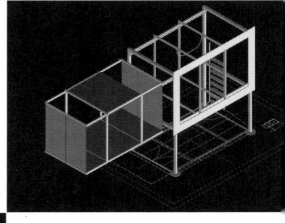

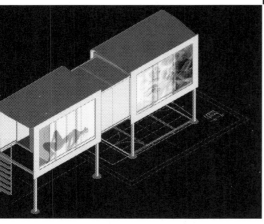

Dome

Shigeru Ban's *Dome* is a cardboard building that does duty as a temporary theatre. Constructed of cardboard tubes clad with a membrane of transparent coated polyester fibre, the geodesic dome has a diameter of 26 m and a maximum height of 10 m. Lightweight and easily disassembled, the construction sits on a sheet steel foundation.

Inside the dome are an auditorium and an oak sculpture by Klaas Kamphuis sunk in the ground. Sea containers serve as storage space and contain the toilets.

Shigeru Ban developed the *Dome* for De Groep Van Steen, a movement theatre company, for an open-air performance at IJburg, the vast expanse of sand in the waters of IJmeer near Amsterdam where a new residential district is in the making.

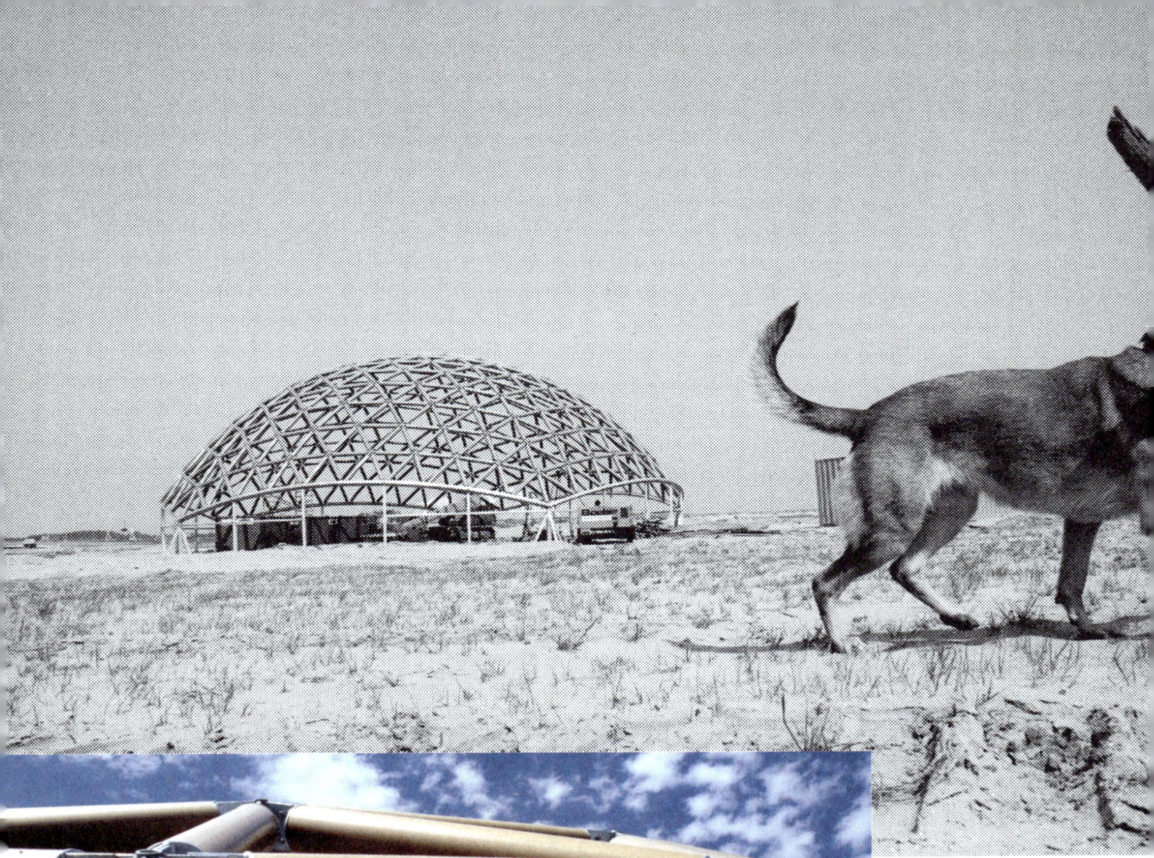

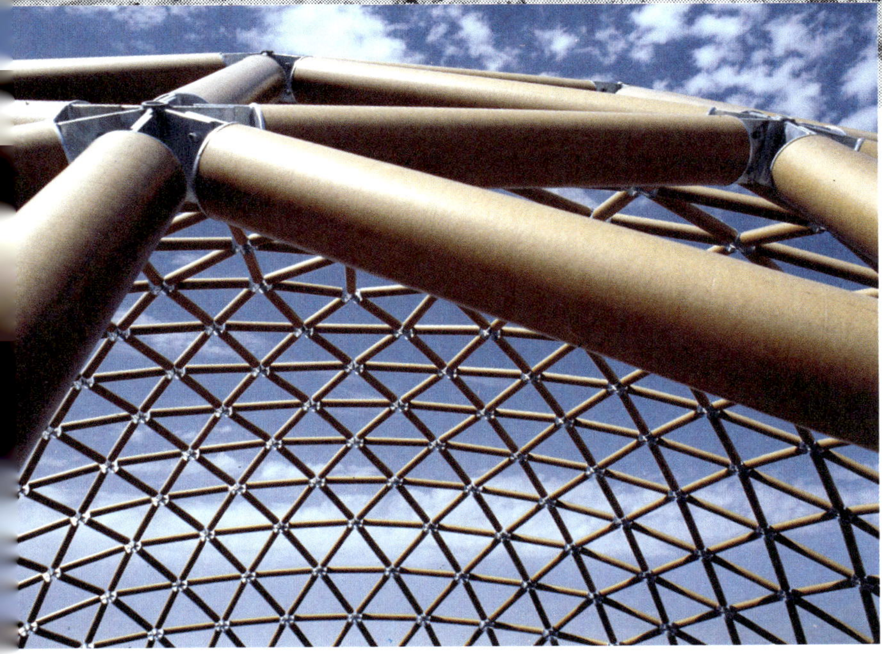

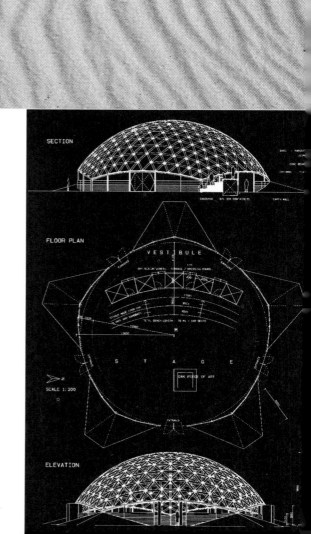

Mobile Porch

Mobile Porch is a mobile mini-architectural object, meant for roaming through public open space. The German artist and architect duo Böhm and Saffer and the architect Andreas Lang designed *Mobile Porch* for the North Kensington Amenity Trust in London. Georgia Ward, the public art consultant for the Trust, invited them to make a temporary project for under the flyover of the Westway in West London. Instead of a static artwork, Böhm, Saffer and Lang developed a mobile urban 'toy', as Kathrin Böhm calls it, meant as a 'place' that the public can use in many ways, ranging from a picnic site to a shop, and from an arts platform to a bar.

Mobile Porch is more than an object. It is a project in which its designers mentally engage with the users and guardians of public space; they see it as a tool for lightheartedly exploring and activating public open space. Their findings can be a valuable source of information about day-to-day activity and for developing strategies for the future. In that sense it is every bit as much a planning tool.

In structural terms *Mobile Porch* is an aluminium drum clad in triplex with a diameter of 2.3 m and a length of 2.1 m. The drum sits on two wheels and is small and light enough for two people to move. The wheels can be removed to make the floor surface larger, and the panels can be variously folded out from the drum.

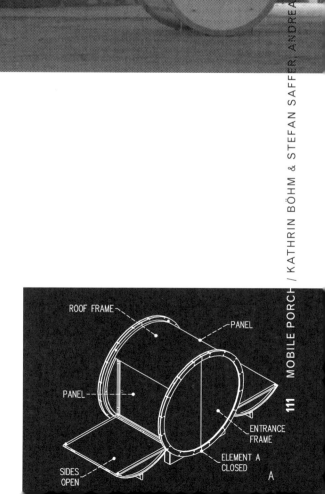

ROOF FRAME

PANEL

PANEL

ENTRANCE FRAME

ELEMENT A CLOSED

SIDES OPEN

A

SUPPORT TUBE

PANEL

SUPPORT TUBE

PANEL

ELEMENT A
OPEN

B

MOBILE PORCH / KATHRIN BÖHM & STEFAN SAFFER / ANDREAS LANG / 2000

MOBILE PORCH / KATHRIN BÖHM & STEFAN SAFFER, ANDREAS LANG / 2000

Miele ruimtestation

2012 Architecten is a small Rotterdam-based firm that makes designs at a variety of scales – graphic design, lighting, furniture, interiors, buildings – producing them itself whenever possible. The team's basic premise is to build upon the potential that is already there, say by taking an existing building, source of energy, or waste matter and transforming it in the design.

In a move to elevate waste to building material 2012 Architecten established what they call 'Recyclicity'. The aim of Recyclicity is to give a new building application to waste using as little added energy as possible. Waste in this case being materials and plant as well as vacant buildings and urban residual space. The use of energy for transport is limited by doing all the work locally.

2012 Architecten are building a website to be able to exchange information about waste materials; they also initiate recycling stations – workplaces temporarily housed in vacant properties – to experiment with local waste flows.

The *Miele ruimtestation* (Miele space station) is an architectural installation made entirely of washing machines, hence the name. This multifunctional mobile unit is compounded out of five separate modules, each of which can be carried by two people. Washing machines have a standard width of 60 cm, and, accordingly, so do these segments. The modules can be rolled through a standard door of 210 x 70 cm. To facilitate transportation the five portions can be assembled on a trailer as a caravan. Once on site, the segments can be placed in various configurations so that the object can be used for many purposes and in different sizes. The space station has already done duty as a bar cum art vending machine, a pavement café and a music shop/office/bar; during 'Parasite Paradise' it serves as a mobile architects' office.

In the context of 'Parasite Paradise' the space station acts as a laboratory for doing research into turning waste flows produced before, during and after construction of a new district to that district's own advantage. This it does by conducting experiments and carrying out commissioned tasks in situ.

During transportation the mobile office is made as compact as possible. It consists of the 'caravan' pulled by a pick-up truck with a five-man cabin. Even in transport mode, the mobile unit can be used as an office and is also suitable for brief 'working visits'. The truck pulling the trailer carries the bridging pieces. For larger projects the space station is expanded using these pieces into an encampment some 20 m long. The modules contain all the hardware: storage, kitchen/shower/toilet, electronics, archive. The flexible lightweight bridging pieces slot between the modules as rooms for dwelling, conferring and working. So as to function entirely unaided, the station provides its own energy (wind turbine and solar energy), generates its own heat (a greenhouse, solar cooker and solar boiler) and has its own water system (water collection and compost toilet).

Lichtspielhaus

It was during a stay at the Künstlerhaus Bethanien in Berlin in 1998 that Wolfgang Winter and Berthold Hörbelt developed their *Lichtspielhaus*, a cinema 25 m long and 10 m wide. The walls of the *Lichtspielhaus* were constructed from 2500 brown bottle crates. Inside, a hundred or so folding chairs funded by the British Council in Berlin filled the space. Every evening during the summer months a trio of projectors showed films made by artists during the past 20 years. The projectors, suitable for different types of films, stood in a special container behind the *Lichtspielhaus*. After the showing there were public discussions about the films, often in the presence of the artists who made them. Drinks could be bought at a kiosk at the entrance.

For 'Parasite Paradise' in Leidsche Rijn Winter & Hörbelt made two proposals, one of which was chosen (though which of the two was not known at the time of going to press). The first was for a new *Lichtspielhaus* that could also accommodate theatre and dance performances. The artists' intention was to create a place where people could meet, engage in conversation and do things together. The other proposal was for 'Utrecht Airport'. Many spatial planners see the ever increasing congestion of vehicular traffic and the relative inaccessibility of railway stations as a reason to stimulate air traffic. Winter/ Hörbelt proposed erecting for the duration of the event in Leidsche Rijn a small hangar for a Fokker plane and a control tower, both entirely of yellow bottle crates, with the public highway doing temporary duty as a runway. Visitors to the event could be taken on a flight over the city of Utrecht.

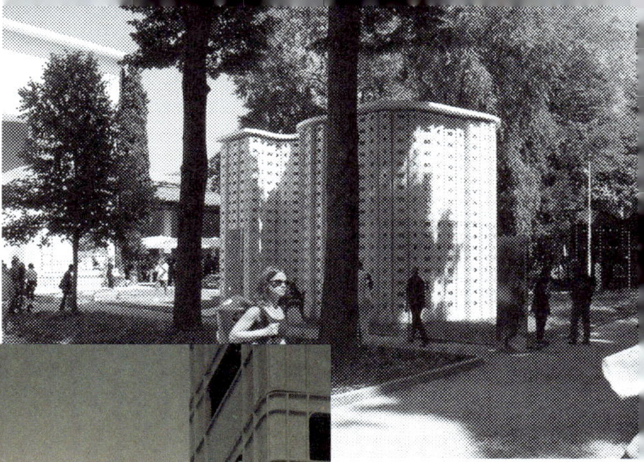

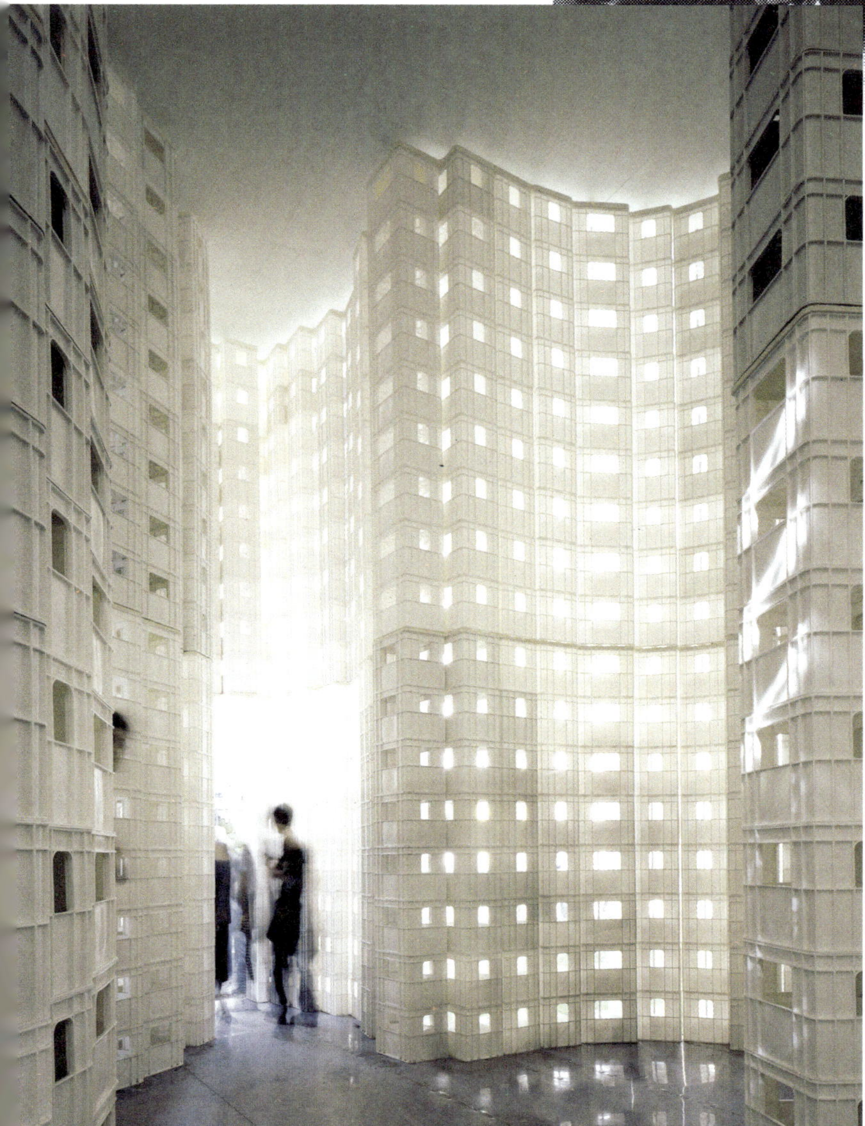

 LICHTSPIELHAUS / WOLFGANG WINTER & BERTHOLD HÖRBELT / 1998

LICHTSPIELHAUS / WOLFGANG WINTER & BERTHOLD HÖRBELT / 1998

Dodenbivak

Dré Wapenaar's *Dodenbivak* (literally, tent for a dead person) is a space where you can take your time in paying your last respects to a loved one or friend.

Dré Wapenaar hopes that his tents will orchestrate and influence meetings between people. *Dodenbivak* is one in a new series of sculptural tents whose theme is the rapport between individuals and groups. This series sees Wapenaar exploring the relationships between attraction and repulsion, intimacy and aloofness, respect and disrespect, and whether these are prompted consciously or unconsciously. *Dodenbivak* translates these pairs of antithetical concepts into a 'heavy' and a light side. The seriousness of death contrasts with the apparent lightness of the funnel-shaped tent. There are no diagonals and the canvas is semi-transparent. The bier is hung from corners that don't seem to be there.

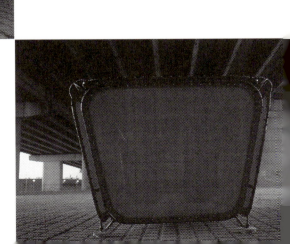

Agora Phobia (digitalis)

Since 2000 an inflatable semi-transparent 'isolation pillar' has been regularly cropping up in crowded public places. This isolation pillar is 3.5 m high with a 2.5 m section and is just large enough to accommodate one person and a computer. Inside the pillar, you feel the physical presence of people outside very strongly, though they can only be vaguely seen. In the intimate space, visitors feel safe and at the same time profoundly vulnerable due to the lack of contact with that external environment.

The computer program allows the visitor to enter into dialogue with people leading isolated existences elsewhere, such as someone in prison, a monk, an asylum seeker, a 'digipersona' or someone suffering from agoraphobia (a morbid fear of open spaces). The dialogues are stored on www.agora-phobia-digitalis.org, where monologues can also be published. *Agora Phobia (digitalis)* of Karen Lancel provides an isolated space for communication where the notions of 'inside' and 'outside' are interchangeable and experiences of insecurity and isolation are explored.

> *Agora Phobia (digitalis)* was shown in the exhibition
> 'Unlimited.nl-3' on Rokin, Amsterdam (2000) at
> the invitation of De Appel, and in Alexanderplatz,
> Berlin (2001) at the invitation of Artfair for Podewil.

Mobile

André van Bergen's *Mobile* is a movable house in the form of a small village. The house consists of eight discrete units on an undercarriage of trailers. The shower, toilet and passage comprise one wagon, the bedroom comprises two wagons and the living/workroom three. The units can be hitched together in various ways, giving rise to the idea of a cluster of cottages or a tiny village. To facilitate deciding how to link them, the units are left open at one side. The exterior of the wagons is of wood and the interior has a standard finish. The kitchen unit stands in the living room.

Forming the basis of the design are the trailers which adhere to a module of 1.5 m. There are four trailers of 4.5 x 1.5 m for the workroom and the passage, two of 1.5 x 1.5 for the shower and toilet and two of 3 x 1.5 for the bedroom. The trailers can be transported by road. Strung together in a row they present a caravan and evoke associations with the movement of nomads or gypsies. Just their movement through space can constitute an event in itself.

Van Bergen sought the simplest possible construction combined with the greatest possible mobility. The house in fact consists of wagons on wheels and so can be transported easily. Since the units can be combined in different constellations, the house can be adapted to suit its setting. Van Bergen deliberately refrained from supplying a vehicle to pull it, for – as he puts it in his project statement - 'for me a real gypsy encampment is one without Mercedes-Benzes, and a real nomad camp one without horses.'

This project was developed for the invited competition held in connection with the exhibition 'Mobile Architecture for Stork', organized in 2001 by SKOR and the Amsterdam Arts Foundation at the former Stork grounds in Amsterdam. On that occasion a number of artists were asked to design a mobile house. The railway lines on site inspired Van Bergen to design a home assembled from mobile units that can also be construed as railway carriages.

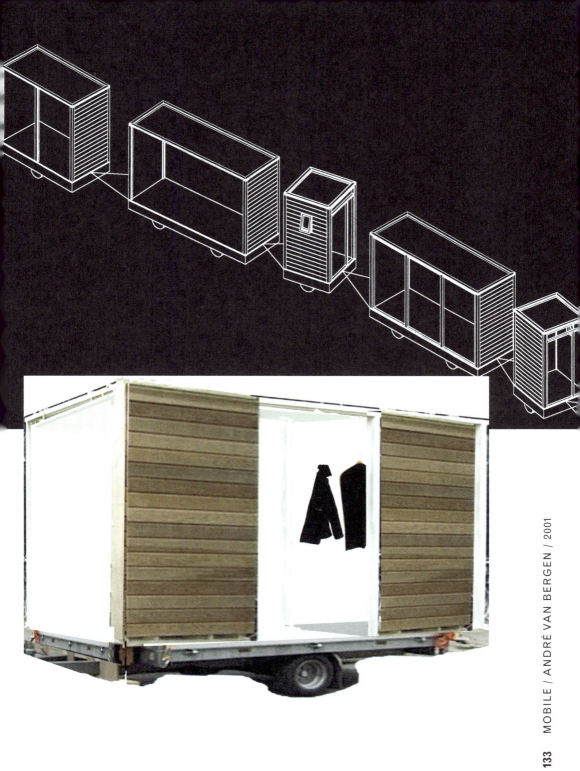

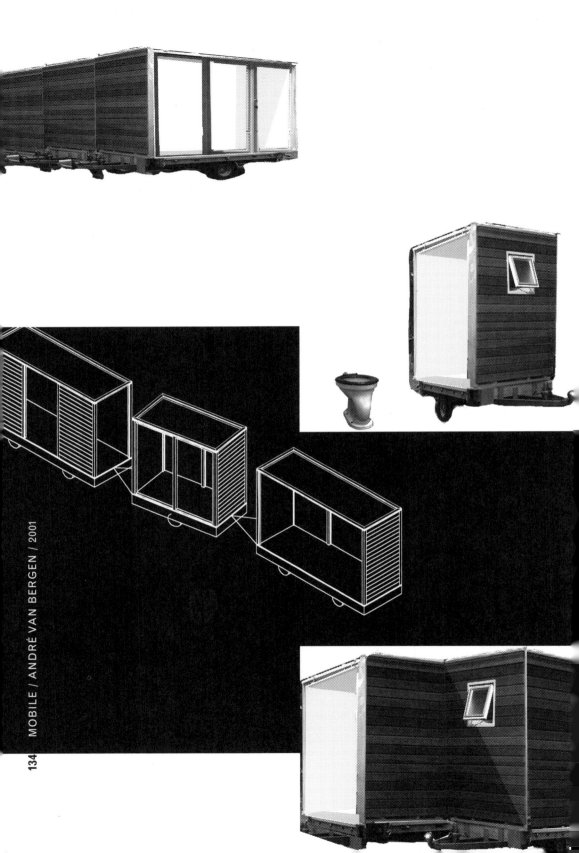

Mobile Unit-shed

Mobile Unit-shed consists of two containers (6 x 2.9 x 2.4 m) in juxtaposition, a sanitary unit (2.3 x 2.4 x 2.5 m), a camper, a wooden platform, and a roof of parasols stitching the components together. The two rust-brown steel sea containers can act as the living quarters: wood clad on the inside, they provide running water, electricity, a toilet, a kitchen and central heating. Held aloft on bamboo canes, the canopy of parasols is illuminated internally at night. The hard tops of the containers can act as an observation point. The camper can serve a variety of purposes and is an essential element for installing and dismantling the mobile unit. Clad internally with wood, velvet and fur, it contains a bed and a TV.

Daniel Milohnic and Dirk Paschke, with Lex Rijkers and Steffi Harzbecher, proceeded from two points of departure. The unit had to be at once functional and sculptural. The combination of containers and parasols is ambivalent too. The containers recall standard industrial architecture whereas the tent-shape of the parasols refers to the nomadic context. Again, the colours and embroidery of the traditional Chinese parasols contrast with the functional containers. These additionally allude to the long distance the parasols have had to travel, from Asia to Amsterdam.

The containers are easy to transport and place. The camper can help in pulling apart the structure supporting the platform and the small sanitation unit.

The easy-to-assemble structure bearing up the parasol roof consists of a frame of bamboo canes in special holders. A combination of bamboo canes and rope takes care of the transverse stability using a traditional Asian knotting technique.

One grasp is enough to open or close the parasols using a system of rods and hooks, the way a sexton snuffs out candles in a church. It doesn't only look elegant, it is functional in emergencies, say if a storm approaches or the wind gets too strong.

This project was developed for the invited competition held in connection with the exhibition 'Mobile Architecture for Stork', organized in 2001 by SKOR and the Amsterdam Arts Foundation at the former Stork grounds in Amsterdam.

chinese umbrella
140 cm diameter

pedestral/outlook

wooden plank 20 x 2 cm
square timber 20 x 10 cm
IPE 20

roof hatch

3,25

2,85

fluorescent lamp

hinged door/
isolated

plywood on square timber
with isolation (10cm)

container/klapptür

bamboo girder
8cm diameter

light switch

window panel

wooden plank
square timber
10 cm x 20 cm

plug

wooden plank on
square timber with
isolation

base plate
10 cm

0,06

small entrance
pedestral

waste   fresh

water supply tanks

prefab foundation
40 x 40 x 100 cm

0,30

PHANTOMBUERO

small wooden
entrance pedestral

window panel
~ 2.50 x 2.50 m

bamboo ladder

reinforced
girder

hinged door /
isolated

plug socket

hinged door /
isolated

delivery/
emergenc

bamboo girder
8 cm diameter

floor marterial:
wooden plank

(smoke alarm)

prefab
foundation
40 x 40cm

fire extinguisher

radiator

required floor space
sanitair container
during transport

mobile kitchen unit
with radiator and
waste water sediment

van/side window

air
conditioner/
heater

tv

van/side window

washing basin
with closet

shower

bed

back
door

slide door

wc

hinged
window
30 x 50 cm

438

turnable
tv-set

extra isolation

optional
flexible
rubber connection
van/shed

telescopic
cylinder
foot/steel

Nomads in Residence

Nomads in Residence, designed by Bik VanderPol in cooperation with Korteknie Stuhlmaker architecten, is a mobile live-work space equipped with one or more mobile garden components. It is not just the house that is mobile but the immediate surroundings too. Its design is not based on minimizing weight and size as is customary. On the contrary, the designers sought to maximize its qualities as an appliance and as a place to spend time. 'A large house that can take a few knocks; with fixed walls you can bang nails into. A house that can still be used after six removals and 19 occupants', as they put it in their design account.

The design is rooted in the simplest and most rudimentary space-form: a container measuring 18 x 4 x 3.2 m that can be easily hauled by road and over water. It can be lifted up by crane in its entirety and deposited on a trailer.

The house can be used and inhabited in many different ways; it is living space and studio in one. There is a large table suitable for receiving large numbers of guests and excellent light for doing serious work.

The 'permanent' surroundings consist of a garden on wheels that can be hitched to the work space. The house too gives more of a permanent than a temporary impression. Floors, walls and roof are of thick, solid glued panels of European softwood: sturdy, angular, heavy, insulating and environmentally friendly. The house can be supplied as a complete kit of parts and assembled on site within days. After assembly it is a stable box that can be lifted by crane and moved around without the need for modification or temporary facilities.

The interior consists of a single basic elongated volume that can be divided into various indoor and outdoor spaces using a wooden sliding partition and a glass panel. The facilities (toilet, shower, kitchen, large table) are parked in the space as a single unit.

The supporting timber panels have a rainproof cladding. The softwood panels are black tarred like a barn; the only dash of colour is the striking fluorescent house number. Part of the roof can be reached from inside as a roof terrace. The remainder is covered in mosses of differing colours: warm in winter, cool in summer.

Inside the house, the wood has a transparent white finish. The large hatches are coated with a vividly coloured scratch and waterproof mock-concrete finish: when the hatches are closed they form large vertical colour planes, when open they become terraces, ramps and stages.

This project was developed for the invited competition held in connection with the exhibition 'Mobile Architecture for Stork', organized in 2001 by SKOR and the Amsterdam Arts Foundation at the former Stork grounds in Amsterdam.

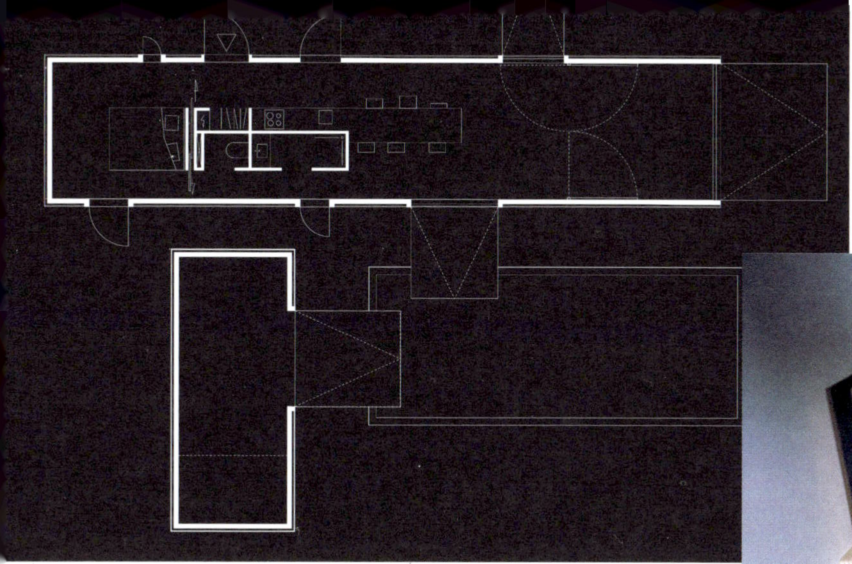

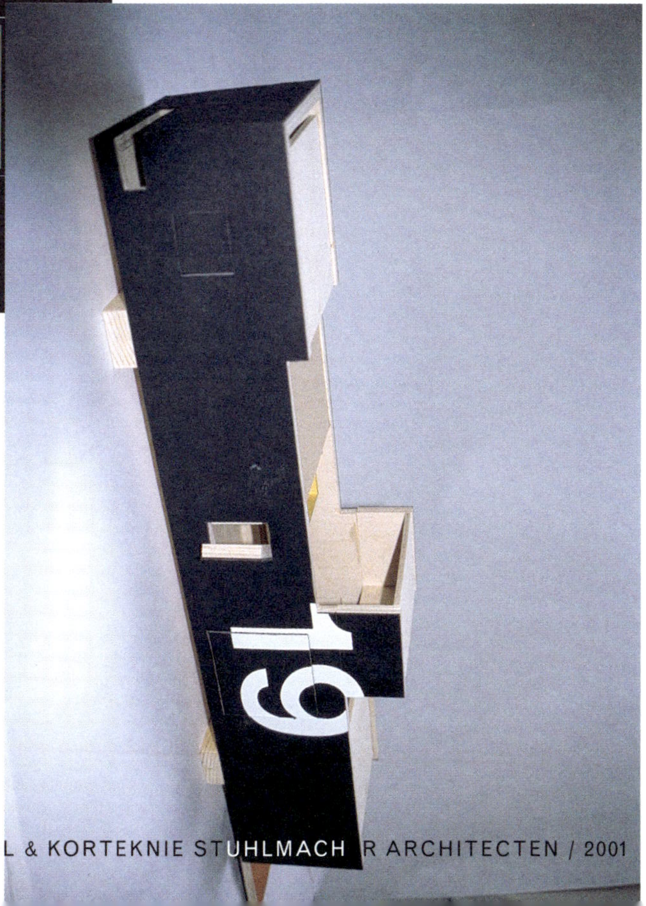

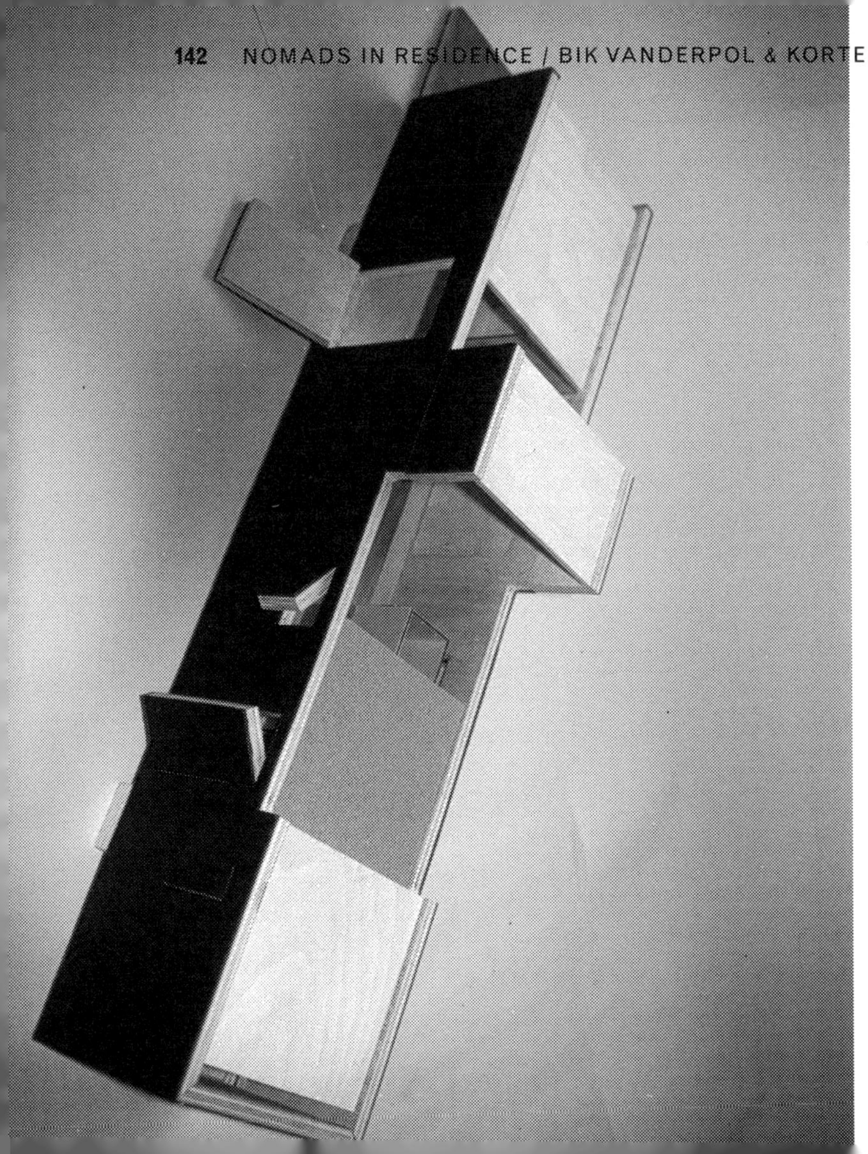

Sainte Bazeille

Sainte Bazeille – the name comes from a lorry that happened to pass by – is a mobile unit that can be used as a house and studio for an artist. The project of Dominique Gonzales-Foerster and Martial Galfione combines an industrial container and a cylindrical silo. The container accommodates the work space and the silo slicing through it at right angles the kitchen, toilet, bathroom and bedroom. Continuing the rear of the silo is a wooden terrace.

The units can be transported by lorry and assembled on site using a crane. They sit on a supporting metal frame which holds them 1.2 metres clear of the ground.

The interior is clad with the bare necessities and has a special lighting system as well as an industrial ventilation system installed inside the container and silo. All elements are off-the-peg with only a few minor changes. It is possible to hitch several units together and expand the whole into a small village.

This project was developed for the invited competition held in connection with the exhibition 'Mobile Architecture for Stork', organized in 2001 by SKOR and the Amsterdam Arts Foundation at the former Stork grounds in Amsterdam.

tube fluo
fixation sur traverses
acier verrière

ouverture dans paroi
du container Ø2.20m

verrière double vitrage 2x 10mm

2.036

seuil en tôle larmée

panneaux contreplaqués sur profil IPN 120mm
+ isolation laine de roche

isolant sur sangles caoutchouc

étagères en métal galva prof. 40cm
fixées sur équerres

2.425

2.660

0.102

0.700

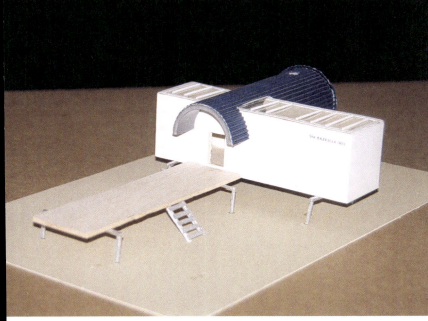

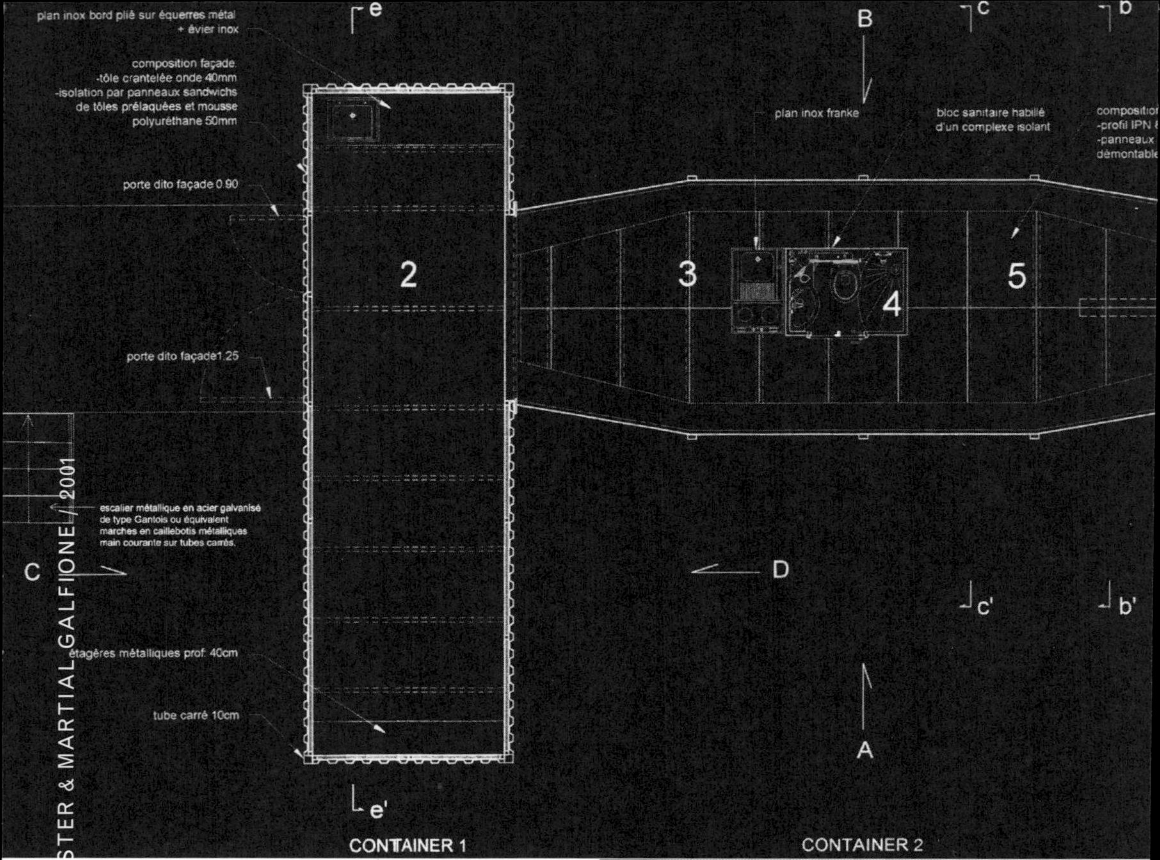

plan inox bord plié sur équerres métal
+ évier inox

composition façade:
-tôle crantelée onde 40mm
-isolation par panneaux sandwichs
de tôles prélaquées et mousse
polyuréthane 50mm

porte dito façade 0.90

porte dito façade1.25

escalier métallique en acier galvanisé
de type Gantois ou équivalent
marches en caillebotis métalliques
main courante sur tubes carrés.

étagères métalliques prof: 40cm

tube carré 10cm

B

┐c   ┐b

plan inox franke   bloc sanitaire habillé   compositio
d'un complexe isolant   -profil IPN
-panneaux
démontable

2   3   4   5

C

D

⌐c'   ⌐b'

A

└e'

CONTAINER 1   CONTAINER 2

MOBILE ARCHITECTUR
CENTURY

Buildings generally are inert, massive, permanent and static. Yet the 20th century has seen the emergence of a great many that are the very opposite, that are relocatable, mobile, demountable, lightweight, portable, temporary, variable, movable and/or flexible. This mobile architecture covers the widest area, from site construction shed to circus tent, from caravan to prefab, from articles of clothing to modular constructional systems, from furniture to recreational vehicles and from ready-mades like cardboard boxes and sea containers to office environments reduced to its portable components: laptop, palmtop and mobile phone.

Anyone so disposed can give the history of mobile architecture an impressive length by going back to the moment in prehistoric times when man traded his shelter of cave and lair for lightweight tents and huts, such as are used to this day by nomadic peoples the world over. Now that the majority of us have moved on to a more sedentary mode of dwelling, mobile architecture has melted into the background, even though there has always been a need for transportable and demountable homes, say for military purposes, expeditions of discovery and trade, and celebrations and festivals. Indeed, we can trace a line right up to the present. But although mobile architecture belongs to every age, it only broke out in a big way in the 20th century, an era pre-eminently in thrall to change and motion. In that century, man's operational range swelled on every front, in social as well as physical mobility. Architects and other designers have attempted to adapt buildings to meet this change in different ways.

Mobility in the 20th century is most indelibly linked with the automobile. The breakthrough and furious growth of automobility and car ownership have played a role in the proliferation of mobile architecture that can scarcely be overestimated. In comparison all other modes of transport pale in significance, from the ocean liners that fired Le Corbusier to the real and imaginary spacecraft that have fascinated so many architects during the past hundred years. Not only has the car itself given rise to diverse forms of mobile architecture – caravans and campers spring immediately to mind – it has served as a source of inspiration and analogy for an architecture determined to shake off its own inertia. This may of course be only figuratively, for example with a stream-lined design suggesting dynamism as the Italian Futurists had wielded back in the 1910s and which became popular in the USA in the following two decades when it was applied to architecture, furniture and daily use objects.

Additionally, the 20th century saw the emergence of a great many forms of architecture and urbanism specifically tailored to the automobile, ranging from concrete structures such as motorways, drive-in homes, multi-storey car parks, filling stations and motels to urban design concepts such as Hans Reichow's *autogerechte Stadt* of the 1950s, Willem Jan Neute-lings' *Ringcultuur* of the '80s and the 'mobility aesthetics' propagated by Francine Houben on the threshold of the 21st century.

Another influence on mobile architecture, if by a circuitous route, is the way cars are produced. Many modern architects treat the car as a paradigm because of its industrialized assembly process and mass production. The functionalists' efforts to achieve an analogous industrial production of archi-tecture was informed by their desire to free architecture from artistic caprice and make it fully functional. The idea arose that if the building industry were to be successfully industrial-ized, the standardization and modular coordination that came with it would enable production of a kit-of-parts architecture. This did not need necessarily to be static formwise but could be flexible and maybe even demountable and in that sense meet the mobile lifestyles and changing needs of modern man. There was also the fact that the war industry, headed by the aircraft factories, was forced to plot a new course in post-war peacetime, particularly in the USA. Even more than the car industry, it sought to contribute to the industrialization of housing. Though exploiting the production methods of aircraft

HANS IBELINGS

construction, there was no attempt made to transfer the aircraft's visual form to housing.

The history of mobile architecture in the 20th century follows two paths. One has been pretty exhaustively documented and canonized in the history of architecture as a whole, and involves artists and industrial designers as well as architects. This history begins shortly after 1900 and standardly includes the likes of Antonio Sant'Elia's futuristic fantasies, Le Corbusier's fascination with automobiles, aircraft and passenger ships, Richard Buckminster Fuller's *Dymaxion House* and *Dymaxion Car* of the 1930s, the pre- and postwar steel houses of Jean Prouvé, the growing and moving cities envisioned by the Japanese Metabolists in the '50s, Archigram's *Walking Cities* of the '60s, up to and including the vehicular and pod-like buildings of Future Systems and Kas Oosterhuis's dynamic architecture. For most mobile or quasi-mobile architecture of this order it holds that it was never put into practice or got no further than the prototype stage. Nor would it have been particularly reasonable in most cases to expect that such schemes would ever be realized. They are either too ambitious or simply too remote from reality. If the truth be told, most projects from this strand of history are for this reason more *illustrations* of mobility than concrete steps towards mobilizing architecture.

The second strand is given up to mobile architecture that has actually been built. It is informed not by noble ideals but much more by motives of practicality. Often it is of secondary importance whether the results look good. In this strand it is not always clear where the dividing line falls between vehicle and built structure, between mode of transportation and space to linger, and whether the designer concerned – assuming he or she can be identified – should be described as an architect or an artist. Is a camper a vehicle with an architectural side, or an architectural object you can drive? And how do you categorize a stretched limo with a sunken sitting area for passengers with a bar and TV? There are many such hybrid forms of architecture and land or water vehicles, from the Renault Espace to the residential units in mobile home parks – mobile only in name these days.

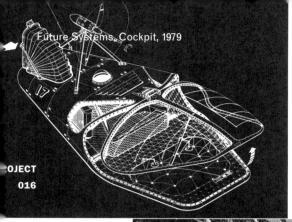

Future Systems, Cockpit, 1979

PROJECT 016

Future Systems, Une petite maison, 1982

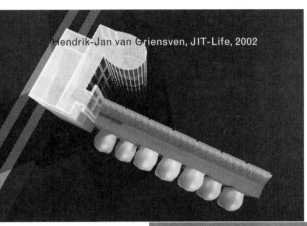

Hendrik-Jan van Griensven, JIT-Life, 2002

Hendrik-Jan van Griensven, JIT-Life, 2002

Mobile architecture belonging to this second strand is informed by restraint and matter-of-factness. It gets produced because there is a market for it: Portakabins, snack carts, hotdog carts, mobile hospitals, party tents, mobile urinals, kiosks, temporary shops, market stalls, exhibition pavilions, sponsor villages, temporary schools, fairground attractions, the list is endless. These forms of mobile architecture satisfy real functional needs without involving exalted ideals for a future society where – as has been proclaimed for the past three quarters of a century or more – we shall lead a nomadic and flexible existence of our own free will. This picture of the future is evidently as persistent as it is unattainable. Back in the 1920s Ludwig Hilberseimer envisaged a near future where everyone would live in hotel-like surroundings; in the 1950s Constant's *New Babylon* project showed man as a player, freed from work and possessions, roaming through new urban structures; and to this very day the idea lives that modern man can manage without a fixed residence or place of belonging. Take the 'JIT-Life' exhibition (subtitled 'the "City" is my home!') held at the Architectuurcentrum in Nijmegen at the beginning of 2003. It features Hendrik-Jan van Griensven's final year project from Tilburg Academy of Architecture, 'a future perspective on nomadic life in the city' rooted in folding, transportable units which could conceivably also serve to provide humanitarian aid during wars and natural disasters.

In the April 2003 edition of Architectuur Lokaal's quarterly journal, Arjen de Groot describes Van Griensven's Just-In-Time-Life as 'requiring a switch in thinking about dwelling' and this is where the problem lies: much high-pitched mobile architecture is not the answer to a manifest need. This is where it differs fundamentally from the world of Portakabin and De Meeuw, whose products have proved to be just that.

If each new description of the history of mobile architecture confirms and perpetuates the idealistic strand, it systematically ignores the pragmatic strand or so it seems. This second history of mobile architecture has never had a coherent clearly unfolding narrative, for the simple reason that no-one has ever done any real research into it. As a result, it is still little more than a disordered assemblage of discrete fragments of architecture that seek not so much to articulate the *idea* of mobility – unlike most of the projects firmly ensconced in the canonized history – but are mobile, flexible and fully relocatable.

Obscure though this strand may be, there is plenty of evidence that the discoveries in this second category are often years ahead of the more famous counterparts among their canonized brethren, which in many cases are reinventions of wheels from way back or existing artefacts appropriated from elsewhere and relabelled architecture. An example of the last-named category is the sea container, which took on its standard form of 20 by 40 feet in the 1950s. Divested of its original purpose, it steadily burgeoned in the 1970s and '80s into a symbol of flexible and mobile architecture. A familiar reinvented wheel is the caravan. It was in about 1920 that this vehicle assumed the form we still know it by today, with Fleming Williams, a British pilot in the First World War, a possible contender for that honour with what he called the Car Cruiser. Yet in 1940 Richard Buckminster Fuller coolly presented the design for a *Mechanical Wing*, a transportable object with one axis that could be hitched to a car, and essentially nothing other than a caravan full of household appliances. The main difference between it and a caravan is that Fuller's *Mechanical Wing* had no sleeping quarters. A more recent example is Eduard Böthlingk's *Markies* which despite all the hoopla is little more than an improved and elegant take on the folding caravan.

All century there has been a glaring discrepancy between the two strands in the history of mobile architecture. At the end of the 1920s, famous modernists like Walter Gropius were full of talk about industrializing and standardizing in the building industry although it had made little headway in practice. Yet the Dutch company of De Meeuw, one of the major producers of temporary buildings, or of IFD construction (Industrial, Flexible and Demountable) as the firm has it these days, had been founded back in 1929. This same De Meeuw held a competition in 2001 among architects to design a building using their IFD system in an attempt to bridge the chasm still separating the two strands of mobile architecture.

In the light of this discrepancy it is easy to understand why Jan Kaplicky of Future Systems included among the flood of images in the first monograph devoted to the firm the Certificate of Recognition that NASA had awarded him in 1989 'for the disclosure of an inventive contribution entitled SPACE STATION WARDROOM

TABLE'. Proof at last that architecture is indeed able to contribute to mobile architecture.

Kaplicky received the certificate shortly after ending his collaboration with David Nixon, the driving force behind Future Systems's quest for potential technological spin-offs for architecture in the rapid advances in the vehicle sector. In the early '80s, Nixon wrote the following in the manifesto *Constructing the Future*: 'Future Systems believes that borrowing technology developed from structures designed to travel across land (automotive), or through water (marine), air (aviation) or vacuum (space) can help to give energy to the spirit of architecture by introducing a new generation of buildings which are efficient, versatile and exciting. This approach to the shaping of the future of architecture is based upon the celebration of technology.'

That architecture was mobile, or in view of the references could look mobile, for Dixon seemed to be of secondary importance, yet it has proved essential for Kaplicky, who carried on with Future Systems when Dixon decided to devote all his time to designing for the American space travel industry. Kaplicky himself designed countless capsule-like buildings whose forms unmistakably allude to space travel. They can be attributed with much the same symbolism as that of the mini-golf obstacle he designed before fleeing Czechoslovakia as an evocation of an 'American way of life'.

The popularity of capsules in the canonized strand of mobile architecture can be directly related to the NASA space travel programme, which had a greater impact on the 'Free West' than the Soviet space programme with its less flashy design. At the close of the 1960s the Space Age not only influenced fashion and watch design but gave us architecture that smacked of space travel and the science fiction of flying saucers. Not only did these capsules refer to the most advanced and innovative form of mobility of the day. Part of their success was certainly due to the suggestion that such capsules, equipped with sundry electrical appliances and gadgets, could provide the basis for a wholly self-sufficient existence – a theme that has always underscored the history of mobile architecture. (A comparable compact mobile architecture in the world of shipping had obviously been around for very much longer, but a saloon, galley or cabin was hardly in the same league as the seductive appearance of an Apollo.) Space-age architecture with its streamlined forms lent itself admirably to production in one of the new synthetic materials. Plastics, which had been developed since the 1950s, looked set for a great future and was to pave the way for a modular architecture, which in all its simplicity seemed to bring the ideal of industrially produced buildings closer than ever. The new plastics opened the doors for another type of mobile architecture in the form of inflatable buildings. The intensive experimenting done in this field in that same period yielded at least one lasting result, the common-or-garden inflatable 'bubble' for covering tennis courts in winter. Yet this period of experimenting with plastic architecture was short-lived, partly due to the sharp rise in the price of plastics following the oil crisis of 1973. The most memorable results were capsule houses such as the American-made *Monsanto* of 1957 (which did duty for ten years as the 'House of the Future' in Disneyland, Anaheim CA) and some European projects largely done in the 1960s, with resounding names like *Rondo*, *Orion*, *fg 2000* and *Futuro*. The climax and at the same time the conclusion of this plastics culture was 'IKA '71', the world's first international plastic housing exhibition held in Lüdenscheid in 1971. Ultimately none of the pieces shown there made good the promise of large-scale housing production.

So nothing ever came of the plans they had in the '60s to build entire villages of such capsules, maybe even underwater. (This was not only the closest approach on earth to life beyond the atmosphere but was seriously considered at the time as a solution for overpopulation on land.) None of this took place, though there were occasions when capsules were attached to buildings, the most successful example being Kisho Kurokawa's Nakagin tower, built in Tokyo in 1972. It consists of a vertical circulation core clipped onto which are comfortable if tiny *existenzminimum* 'bachelor capsules'. Although theoretically extendible in every direction, this has not been the case in practice. Herein lies one of the tragedies of this

Kisho Kurokawa, Nakagin capsule tower, Tokyo 1972. Photo Tomio Ohashi

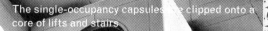

The single-occupancy capsules are clipped onto a core of lifts and stairs

Interior of capsule

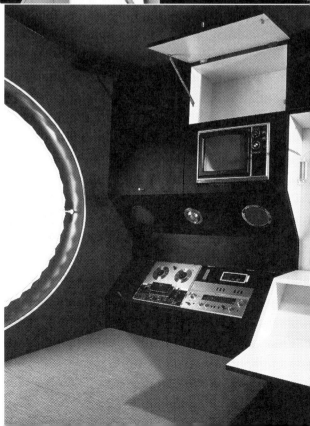

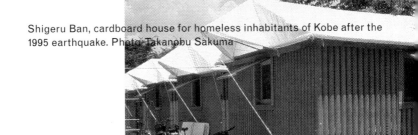

Shigeru Ban, cardboard house for homeless inhabitants of Kobe after the 1995 earthquake. Photo Takanobu Sakuma

Shigeru Ban, cardboard house interior. Photo Hiroyuki Hirai

Shigeru Ban, tent for refugees, United Nations. Photo Shigeru Ban Architects

Krzysztof Wodiczko, *Homeless Vehicle*, New York City, 1988–1989
(Krzysztof exhibited in De Appel, Amsterdam) Photo © Cary Markerink

form of mobile architecture: once built, in most cases its potential mobility failed to materialize, leaving it as inert as the static architecture from which it sought to extricate itself.

Apart from the fact that most architects and artists in the province of mobile architecture have done little more than appropriate the anonymous findings of others and spin-offs from mobility technology, there is one other thing they have in common. Almost all the dreams inherent in the mobile architecture of architects and artists can be traced back to the idea that a life without possessions is liberating. We are then free to do as we please. The autarkic capsule relates to this idea, but so does the notion of nomadism as the highest state of being. Typically, nomads are invariably presented as unattached individuals without anything as bourgeois as a family. (A loner partnered by another loner is only just acceptable, but your genuine mobile type is free of all ties.)

Continuing this line of enquiry, people are freest if they have no baggage in tow. We can expand upon this by adding that they are freer still if they have no need to stick to rules and regulations. This brand of freedom has been professed for decades, by drop-outs in the California desert, free spirits in Christiania in Copenhagen, Amsterdam squatters in the 1970s and '80s and by urban nomads particularly in the '80s and '90s. But this urge for freedom has seldom taken on an architectural dimension, let alone a mobile architectural one. It is only in recent years that this situation has seen change, with projects like *AVL-Ville*, the container and capsule village where Joep van Lieshout elevated the non-observance of rules and regulations to an all-encompassing theme.

In recent years the idea of a possessionless, propertyless nomadism has struck home in the hedonistic quarter, as exemplified by the exhibition 'New Hotels for Global Nomads' curated by Donald Albrecht of the Cooper-Hewitt National Design Museum in New York. Its message is summarized to perfection on the exhibition catalogue's inside flap text: 'The world is on the move: geographic borders have broken down as people can increasingly travel anywhere, anytime, for business and pleasure. The modern hotel accommodates and even encourages this new international nomadism, not only offering a place to sleep, but, through its design, amenities and sense of theatre, providing its guests with the ultimate escapist experience.' The joylessness of a standard hotel room and the pitiful figure of the travelling salesman who is never home have ceded to an element of jealousy towards those who can afford a life of luxury in well-designed hotels.

The pleasure-loving hotel nomad represents one extreme of the spectrum of travelling light: the other is that of the homeless who often have little more than a sheet of cardboard or a blanket as shelter; asylum-seekers confined to makeshift camps, barracks or tents where they wait for the powers that be to decide their fate; and refugees fleeing famine, human violence or natural disasters.

Fortunately, architects have not just targeted the nomadic 'haves' but the 'have-nots' as well, certainly since the 1960s. A number of designers have sought to contribute towards improving the lives of these unwilling nomads. Recently, Shigeru Ban designed buildings constructed of cardboard tubing for the inhabitants of Kobe who had been made homeless by the 1995 earthquake. He also devised tents for refugees at the behest of the United Nations. At the end of the '80s Krzysztof Wodiczko developed a *Homeless Vehicle* for the destitute of New York. Resembling a cross between a shopping trolley and a wastebasket, this vehicle can carry their scant possessions and collected deposit cans. It pulls out into a safe, securable sleeping place. In the 1970s Hans-Walter Müller, specialist in inflatable architecture, experimented with plastic tents for clochards that could be placed on top of the Paris Métro's ventilation grilles. The warm air inflated the tent and kept its homeless occupant warm and dry. A disadvantage of this sympathetic project was that the tents were so small that you could not lie in them outstretched.

Compared with the lofty ideals architects display in other provinces of mobile architecture, we can expect only modest assistance from them when it comes to the unwillingly mobile among us. As Sanford Ponder, the American inventor of *The Pod*, puts it: 'If we must live in a world in which people are forced to live in cardboard boxes, than someone should at least invent a better box.'

He arrived at this conclusion 'in early 2001, at a point in my life where everything was changing dramatically. The startup company I had been working with had to change its business model to survive the market downturn, which meant the elimination of many positions, including my own. At the same time I had lost a small fortune in my own personal investments. So, I was sitting unemployed, on the sofa, watching a television programme about homeless people

living in little enclaves constructed from corrugated boxes. While contemplating the potential for my own homelessness, the thought occurred to me, if people (or I) have to live in boxes, then someone should invent a better box. I started to cut out paper patterns and here I am.' 'Icosa Village' is his endeavour to bring onto the market a cross between an igloo and a geodesic dome for 'a variety of recreational, promotional, entertainment and humanitarian uses', with the most emphasis on the latter: 'It is our intention to become the preferred supplier of high value, low cost, aesthetically appealing shelter solutions to governmental, NGO, and international relief organizations addressing the worldwide refugee shelter crisis.'

A compromise for those who prove unable to lead a totally possessionless existence is to reduce one's goods and chattels in mass and volume to a manageable, transportable and perhaps even portable minimum. Since the Second World War, efforts in this direction have made enormous advances on the back of miniaturization and digitization, the most spectacular result – with no architects involved – being the reduction of the complete office to a bundle of electronics that easily fits in a shoulder bag. Architects have contributed to this drive to reduction by devising mobile and portable objects that can be construed either as a compressed home or some part of it, or as new multifunctional furnishing units designed to satisfy all the basic necessities of life. Such survival kits were produced in the 1970s by the Dutch architect Arne van Herk, who designed a chest that is at once bed, bench, desk and cupboard, and the industrial designer Joe Colombo who developed the *Total Furnishing Unit*. In the 1980s Toyo Ito advanced a *Dwelling for Tokyo Nomad Women*, a tiny cell, and in the '90s this theme was tackled in a big way by artists like Allen Wexler and Joep van Lieshout. All these build upon a trend that extends back a long way. As early as 1775 Thomas Jefferson had designed for himself a portable writing desk (on which it is claimed he wrote the *Declaration of Independence*) and in the 19th century Louis Vuitton fulfilled similar needs with the secretary-trunk, the collapsible bed-in-a-trunk and other practical travel items. So it was really nothing new, although it seemed a radical move in 1966, when Archigram's Mike Webb presented the *Cushicle*, 'an invention that enables a man to carry a complete environment on his back. It inflates-out when needed. It is a complete nomadic unit – and it is fully serviced. It enables an explorer, wanderer or other itinerant to have a high standard of comfort with a minimum of effort.'

Comfort is the key word in most mobile architecture. At least as important as the quest for mobility is the comfort it is to provide. Without wanting to slap a Freudian reading on it, the predilection for pod-like structures can be explained not only from the desire to be or look mobile. The association with the womb is too obvious an interpretation to ignore.

This brings us to one of the paradoxes of much mobile architecture. Admittedly, it is targeted at people with an unerring sense of direction and at ease wherever they happen to be. But however swashbuckling and mondain these globetrotters may be, mobile architecture offers them a modicum of comfort, warmth and security denied them by the average house since the rise of modernism. The opulent luxury of a hotel makes it more than just a home away from home as the hotel ads themselves often proclaim – it is the very last word in homes. After all, whose own bed is as soft, whose towel as thick and absorbent and whose carpeting as springy as in a five-star hotel? Again, the security and comfort of capsule buildings, even when made of a smooth synthetic material, are a surprisingly close approximation of the womb. Even your average caravan or camper often harbours more domesticity behind its thin fibreglass walls than the proverbial cosy cottage. Within the avant-garde vision of radically transforming man and architecture by letting them escape from their own inertia and disengage, there resides a thoroughly human desire for safety and security that is evidently the destiny of us all.

PORTRAIT OF THE ARTIST AS AN ARCHITECT

Alicia Framis made a bar for women only. Carsten Höller and Rosemarie Trockel built a house for pigs and people. Rirkrit Tiravanija built a kitchen for everyone. Jorge Pardo built a house for himself. Atelier van Lieshout made an entire city. Andrea Zittel designs practical living units; Mariko Mori inhabits space-age pods. Angela Bulloch puts pixel light boxes on building facades while Höller likes to add circular slides. Aernout Mik's video projections are inseparable from the structures he builds for them. Pipilotti Rist projects her videos on floors, kitchen cabinets and living rooms. With her installations, Monica Bonvicini sexualizes architecture while Elmgreen & Dragset re-stage the white cube, adding political layers to its seemingly neutral walls. Michel Majerus and Franz Ackermann make paintings as total environments while Olafur Eliasson brings the environment into buildings. Gregor Schneider continues to rework the *Haus Ur* while Manfred Pernice makes fragmentary structures that are filled with history and holes.

Contemporary artists are increasingly turning to architecture, whether it's to make a video into a video installation, to install an autonomous structure or to transform an existing one. As art works move beyond the confines of the picture frame and take up more space – both within and beyond the walls of the museum – artists have begun to build, sometimes by necessity but more often by choice. While we may marvel at their mixed-media creations, Renaissance figures such as Brunelleschi and Alberti would most likely be surprised to see just how few artists have actually built buildings in their wake. Our inevitable question – 'Is this art or architecture?' – would probably appear to them as a strange, if not impossible, line of inquiry. In the Renaissance view, the two practices were not just complementary but also necessary to each other.

167

Their question to us might be: How can you build if you cannot draw, paint and sculpt? The fusion of skills advocated by the humanists – arts, languages, sciences – reached its apex in formidable figures like Leonardo da Vinci and Michelangelo, who could build a library, paint a fresco or design a flying machine.

In this essay, the question about the relationship between art and architecture will not be expressed as a problem of classification, nor as an argument about skill, craft, technology or even education. Instead, I will try to explain what actually drove the two practices apart – from the perspective of aesthetics. In particular, I want to focus on an epistemological shift in the 18th century that not only differentiated the artist from the architect but also made their works distinct, if not hostile, with respect to each other. The approach is a novel one since many of the discussions about art and architecture tend to document both individuals and movements that managed to unite – not divide – the two practices. There is the vast literature on the Renaissance as well as on the *Gesamtkunstwerk*, first conceptualized by Wagner and reformulated in a variety of ways at the turn of the last century by a wide range of international movements, including Futurism, De Stijl, Bauhaus and Constructivism. While these movements established important precedents, it seems erroneous to ask why art and architecture are getting together once again today without considering how they first fell apart.

Second, I will argue that the roots of the current fusion between art and architecture actually lie in Conceptual Art and develop fully in Relational Aesthetics. Despite the significance of historical precedents, contemporary artists who use architecture do not seem to be concerned with reincarnating the Renaissance *homo universalis* or reviving the *Gesamtkunstwerk* with yet another movement. Their works may be large-scale and multi-media, but they are temporary interventions that seem to be based upon a discrete concept rather than an elaborate philosophy on the aesthetics of living. Artists using architecture today open up a situation within an existing space rather than articulating a world view or even instigating an aesthetic, socio-political programme that could be applied to anywhere, anyone and anything, from the roof to the crockery. Indeed, the total – and totalitarian – gestures of the past century that fused art and architecture in both exceptional and unforgivable ways have become more modest. Today's gestures are fragmentary, parasitic, ephemeral and mobile ones that tend to favour a reciprocal yet open relation with the public. Finally, by taking a closer look at individual contemporary projects – including Atelier van Lieshout's *AVL-Ville* – I will consider how art and architecture are getting along in their most recent attempt at cohabitation.

From Design to Aesthetics

Few will recall the French art historian P. Monier. But Monier is a good point of departure for grasping what was at stake in dividing art from architecture. Monier's 1698 three-volume treatise covers the entire history of the arts – painting, sculpture, architecture, engraving – from their origin to their re-establishment.[1] But where does Monier start? Of course, with Creation. God is the first artist; the world, the first art work – an extra large-scale, multi-media installation that included everything made at the beginning and everything produced afterwards. After God comes Noah who practised the arts of maritime architecture and geometry. Monier continues through the bible, across antiquity and over French history, looking for traces of 'le dessein originel'. In this age, the *cabinet de curiosités* and the *Kunstkammer* – where drawings sat alongside minerals, antiquities and measuring instruments – reflected the belief that God's will was expressed in every creation. One intention – or design – is what held art and architecture firmly together. To divide the two practices would be akin to introducing an uninvited collaborator into the divine plan.

What divided art from architecture was not the emergence of secular narratives in art history – Vasari and Winckelmann come to mind – but aesthetics. In fact, Kant's third critique – *Kritik der Urteilskraft* (1790) – was decisive in segregating art, not only from architecture, but also from traditional crafts and from applied arts, which later falls into the vast category of design. Although Kant has little to say about art and architecture – apart from a few digressions on frames and columns – he manages to divide the two practices by claiming that

169

judgements of taste must be devoid of interest, be it personal, objective or practical.[2] If a given 'presentation' is marked by an interest – Kant uses the term presentation (*Darstellung*) to ensure that aesthetic judgements can be made about anything – then this presentation, however pleasing, cannot be beautiful but remains merely agreeable. Unlike his contemporaries who attempted to define beauty, Kant maintains that there is no determinate concept for beauty. For Kant, beauty cannot be reduced to a particular set of characteristics or objects, nor even to the art object itself. Rather beauty reflects the feeling of pleasure that arises from judging a presentation along with the conviction that everyone else experiences the same pleasure.

After Kant, art and architecture – the artist and the architect – part ways. Art remains in the realm of beauty by virtue of its uselessness, its autonomy, its freedom, which are manifest in the terms 'fine arts' and 'beaux-arts'. Architecture, by contrast, is always marked by a specific purpose and use. Since architecture cannot be judged without interest, it always falls short of beauty. Use excludes not only architecture from beauty but also an endless range of objects – jewellery, books, clothes, linen, furniture, glass, carpets – which had been developed over centuries by artists who were now demoted to the status of artisans, craftsmen or technicians. In the wake of Kant, only the 'useless' elements – the decoration – can be beautiful; the rest is just agreeable. In many ways, Kant is the father of modern design since his restrictions create a stimulus for future designers who attempt to bring together beauty and use, to unite form and function. At the same time, the ever-expanding category of design recalls Monier's 'dessein originel' and expresses a yearning for a lost totality. While art seems to fare well in Kant's system, the absence of a concept for beauty forces art to change constantly or to risk being agreeable or even becoming knowledge. After all, repetition could give rise to a concept that might allow one to define what art is – a situation that would automatically shift art from the realm of aesthetics and beauty to the realm of knowledge. Due to repetition and utility, traditional collective arts are demoted to crafts – doubly excluded by Kantian aesthetics. Architecture, for better or for worse, is left to pursue function, with the option of being agreeable. Unlike art, architecture also seems to exist in a much longer time frame since durability and permanence are understood as part of a building's function. Moreover, architecture can afford to be repetitive and marked by a concept since it can never be more than agreeable. This different relation to time – art as ephemeral, architecture as durable – will prove to be crucial for current attempts to reunite the two practices.

Beyond isolating art, Kantian aesthetics articulates the mechanics of the community created by the public museum, where visitors can assume their pleasure is shared with other visitors. The public museum also replaces the heterogeneous collections of the *cabinet de curiosités* and the *Kunstkammer* with a homogeneous and historical presentation of paintings, sculptures, drawings, prints. Indeed, the museum – a work of architecture built to house works of art – manifests the predicament of dividing the two practices. Take Berlin's Altes Museum, designed by Schinkel and completed in 1830. An architect, painter, designer and inventor, Schinkel not only drew up the plans for the museum but also painted astrology scenes at the entrance. Oddly enough, the plan for a rotunda, which cuts through both floors in the middle of the building, became a point of contention. Schinkel's critics cited the high costs of an unnecessary – and useless – element of grandeur in his design. How can one hang paintings on curved walls? A true Kantian, Schinkel maintained that the rotunda, however ostentatious, was necessary precisely because its grandeur would prepare visitors for looking at art. 'Here the sight of a beautiful and sublime room must make people receptive and create an atmosphere for the enjoyment and the judgement of what the building keeps in the first place,' he claimed, evidently with success.[3] While Schinkel may have won as an architect, the victory actually lies with art. Critics claimed that the rotunda was not useful, but Schinkel argued that its uselessness was crucial to make the building function best. Today, museums tend to include an 'empty' unused space – rotunda, atrium, garden, staircase, promenade, hall – where architecture approaches art, only to become subservient to it, existing discreetly behind the frames and pedestals. The public museum, while protecting art's autonomy, manifests architecture's attempt – and failure – to be judged in the

171

same way as art. Ultimately, the museum is built for the art works; the art works are not made for the building.

From Aesthetics to Concepts

The jump from Kantian aesthetics to Conceptual Art – and over decisive movements such as Constructivism and Bauhaus – is undoubtedly an odd path to follow in order to discover how art and architecture have come back together in the wake of Kant's restrictions. After all, Conceptual Art, however diverse in its expressions, is usually associated with the dematerialization of the art object, to cite Lucy Lippard's concise assessment, and not with art's growth into larger and more tangible forms which might be mistaken for architecture. Indeed, Peter Osborne defines Conceptual Art through a series of negations that seem to depict the art work in a continued state of disintegration: the negation of material objectivity; the negation of medium; the negation of visual form; the negation of established modes of autonomy.[4] Alexander Alberro's definition focuses on expansions that nevertheless depict art as a vanishing act: an expanded critique of the art object's materiality; a growing wariness towards the purely visual; a fusion of the work with site and display contexts; an increased emphasis on the possibilities of publicness and distribution.[5] Whatever definition one chooses, both initially appear to suggest that Conceptual Art had few lessons to offer contemporary artists about architecture.

Yet it is precisely this radical transformation – negations for Osborne, expansions for Alberro – that allowed art to break away from traditional media such as painting and sculpture and, later, to take on unexpected forms, including architecture. Conceptual Art fully liberated the art work – and the artist – from what had become a restrictive and institutionalized ritual, no matter how diverse its manifestations: master a skill to make objects, organize them by media, fabricate them to be seen in silence, exhibit them in the museum or the gallery. Ironically, at least in terms of Kantian aesthetics, Conceptual Art frees art from a determinate concept that threatened to reduce art to knowledge. The concept in Conceptual Art is not a determinate one but a liberatory one that always changes and thus allows art to be anything and to exist anywhere. Far from vanishing, art becomes omnipresent, moving beyond dis-

172

crete objects to inhabit environments, often temporarily, both inside and outside the walls of the museum.

Indeed, the public museum is no longer a golden cage protecting art's autonomy and beauty, but a platform, a site, a stage, a point of intervention, a place for institutional critique, a public space, an empty room, a massive billboard, a distribution system. The 'dematerialization' of the art object not only dissolves the strict division between the architecture of the museum and the art inside but also allows for the museum – along with other buildings – to be integrated within the art work itself. As Alberro argues, the Conceptual work could fuse with site and display contexts as well as seek new forms of distribution and publicness – two strategies that can evidently include architecture. Instead of a fusion, I would suggest a parasitic appropriation, where the artist uses existing architecture as a painter uses a fresh canvas, albeit in a temporary way. Thus, the language works of Joseph Kosuth or Lawrence Weiner may appear quite lean – flattened on a wall – but the sparseness of their interventions emerges only if the walls are not considered as part of the works.[6] Since Conceptual Art was wary of producing discrete objects – like a new building or an independent structure – it's not possible to trace all of today's creations to the movement. Nevertheless, Conceptual Art reunited art and architecture in a unique, if not often antagonistic, manner: parasitic, ephemeral, haphazard.

From Concepts to Relations

While Conceptual Art opened the art object in a way that could include architecture, many other artists also worked with architecture to establish important precedents: Gordon Matta-Clark's cuts, James Lee Byar's living gargoyles, Christo's wrappings, Krzysztof Wodiczko's projections, Daniel Buren's stripes, Mario Merz's igloos, Jenny Holzer's signs, Guillaume Bijl's sets, Keith Haring's graffiti, to name just a few.[7] But the inspiration for contemporary artists to use architecture does not seem to come from a growing tradition of artists working with the 'new' medium of architecture. In any case, such a line of reasoning ignores the possibilities created

173

by Conceptual Art, by forcing art objects back into media, even if these media appear in expanded categories like installation, public art and site-specific work. Instead, I would argue that Relational Aesthetics offered both the inspiration and impetus for contemporary artists to build. Of course, the term 'esthétique relationnelle' was developed by the French critic and curator Nicolas Bourriaud who saw a complex shift in works of the early nineties – works that many continue to describe as simply interactive or even performance art.[8] Key figures include Felix Gonzalez-Torres, who invited visitors to take a poster from a stack or a candy from a pile, and Rirkrit Tiravanija, who invited visitors to eat, hang out, make music, rest. While not directly addressing art and architecture, Bourriaud also discusses the work of several contemporary artists who continue to use architecture today, including Pierre Huyghe, Dominique Gonzalez-Foerster, Liam Gillick, Carsten Höller, Angela Bulloch, Andrea Zittel.

Far from creating simple interactions or staging performances, Relational Aesthetics presents the art work as a series of open relations. For Bourriaud, the movement can be understood as a critical reaction to the rising service industry, which increasingly determines and commercializes social relations, if not the entire public space. Instead of looking – and shopping – spectators are invited to use the art work and even take it away at no cost. Indeed, the Relational work is incomplete without the spectator, who is ultimately transformed into a collaborator and decides how the work will be completed. Thus, Gonzalez-Torres's posters disappear from the museum floor and are carried away to adorn the walls of other buildings; Tiravanija's meals are eaten by guests who then carry the work in their bodies until it is transformed into waste. Since the spectator always acts as a collaborator, these works tend to change and to evolve, often in unforeseeable ways – in contrast to interactive works, like Franz West's *Paßstücke*, or orchestrated performances. Unlike Conceptual Art, Relational Aesthetics is not concerned with melting down the art object, nor with breaking up traditional media, but with facilitating relations beyond economic exchanges. As a result, architec-

Rirkrit Tiravanija, *Untitled*, 1996, Kölnische Kunstverein

Dominique Gonzalez-Foerster, Plan d'Evasion, Documenta 2002

Gregor Schneider, Haus Ur, 1985–2001 Rheydt. Photo Gregor Schneider

Gregor Schneider, Haus Ur, 1985–2001 Rheydt. Photo Gregor Schneider

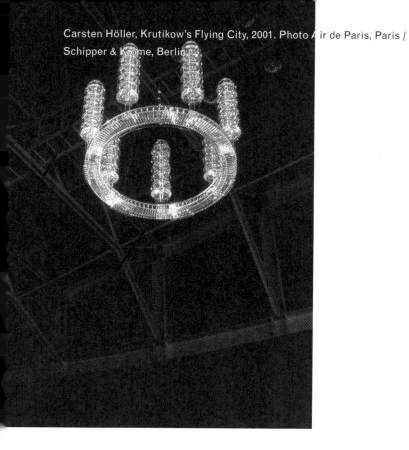

Carsten Höller, Krutikow's Flying City, 2001. Photo Air de Paris, Paris / Schipper & Krome, Berlin

ture – and design – crop up in Relational works as an invitation to the public, a way of establishing contact through familiar forms that spectators trust to enter, without necessarily knowing what to expect. Thus, Gonzalez-Torres did not put his posters on a pedestal but directly on the floor, the only architectural surface in the museum that truly belongs to the visitor. Of course, the endless piles of posters infer other buildings that can only be imagined, both in the past and the future – walls where the posters hang alongside other pictures in an imagined museum. Tiravanija builds temporary platforms, pavilions and rooms where he offers not just meals and a place to relax but also the possibility of meeting other people. Like Gonzalez-Torres's posters, these social contacts may go on – or may not go on – to exist in the architecture of other places.

Where Conceptual Art expands the possibilities for art objects, Relational Aesthetics clearly expands the possibilities for art's audience, integrating the visitor into the art work as a collaborator. Indeed, Relational Aesthetics opens up the role of creator to the extent that the production and reception of the art work become interchangeable and, most importantly, collectivized. Architecture becomes significant for Relational Aesthetics precisely because architecture is inherently collective and relational, from the perspective of both fabrication and use. Like Conceptual Art, Relational works can be parasitic and live off existing buildings, but, since Relational Aesthetics is not reluctant to create material objects, then temporary structures – such as pavilions, platforms, rooms or even tents – are often installed as autonomous structures on, within or outside existing buildings. Indeed, the 'empty' unused spaces of the public museum – from the main hall to the garden – become ideal construction sites. The ephemeral and haphazard also take a new turn in Relational Aesthetics. Visitors may be collaborators, but their numbers – along with their desires and friends – remain as unknown as the way in which they will relate to each other. Human relations add a socio-psychological layer – and therefore an unaccountable dimension – to the work, beyond its immediate materiality. The ephemeral and haphazard lie, not in the art object, but in the people. By welcoming the individual into a shared experience, the architecture in Relational Aesthetics remains suspended between the particular and the collective, the present and

177

an open future. Again, since relations can continue beyond the art work's immediate setting, the architectural forms remain incomplete because they always imply buildings and spaces that can only be imagined. While reformulating the parasitic, the ephemeral and the haphazard, Relational Aesthetics adds a few new qualities to the work of art as architecture: accessible to individuals, used collectively, unplanned, incomplete.

Reuniting Art and Architecture After Kant

Before turning to contemporary works, I would like to consider how Conceptual Art and Relational Aesthetics revise Kantian aesthetics – where art and architecture first parted ways. In Conceptual Art, Kant's limitations on aesthetic judgements – like the interdiction on interest, including use – are evidently overruled, if not eliminated for good. Art can be used without losing the possibility of being judged aesthetically. As Thierry de Duve has argued with Duchamp's ready-mades, the question about a presentation's beauty – which can never be defined – is replaced by the question about whether a presentation is art.[9] Like Kant's beauty, art escapes definition and exists only by being judged by a community. Conceptual Art – while highly indebted to Duchamp, along with Dada and Surrealism – adds a strong institutional critique to its predecessors. In the case of the public museum, art's autonomy is no longer based upon the physical barrier of the museum but is fully guaranteed by community. The architecture of the public museum and the white cube of the commercial gallery are used parasitically but above all critically, since they are viewed as the material form, if not the means, of institutionalized power. While architecture may become the support for any art work, it can also become the object of critique, insofar as a given building is linked with structures of power.

Relational Aesthetics evidently follows suit as far as interest and use are concerned. But more significantly, Relational Aesthetics transforms Kant's aesthetic community – *sensus communis aestheticus* – from an individual experience that is assumed to be shared, into a collective one that can be experienced. Judging subjects finally get to meet each other – not to confirm their judgements (Is this beautiful? Is this art?) but rather to get to know, and, perhaps, to enjoy the community to which they belong. Clearly, there

178

are no limits to using architecture – whether existing or new structures – since architecture is inherently social. Institutional critique persists, but architecture is not only cited for its historical relationship to power. Indeed, the focus on relations means that structures tend to be intimate, making an easy point of entry – whether a door, a hole, a chair, a bed, a couch, a mat – for the individual to get in and encounter others. While the museum and the gallery continue to be the target of critique, it's evident that Relational Aesthetics depends upon the autonomy and freedom of art guaranteed by the architecture of the museum – not art's liberation from use, but its relative liberation from the market. Again, as Bourriaud argues, the movement acts against the colonization of social relations by the service economy along with the spectacle. While art by no means escapes the market, the museum and even the gallery are rare spaces where the public can simply 'loiter'. The fact that most art works in the public museum are not for sale – along with the absence of entrance fees at galleries and many museums – are key elements for artists seeking to explore relations outside the market.[10] The tacit consensus in Kantian aesthetics – the universal communicability of *sensus communis aestheticus* – means that the subjects of aesthetic judgements have never had the need to relate directly to each other; thus they have no predetermined ideas about what to do together, once the silence is broken. As the art object could become anything, here, the relations among judging subjects can be established and experienced in any way. The public museum, an almost 'virgin' space of sociability, becomes an ideal site for Relational works.

What about art and architecture? After Conceptual Art and Relational Aesthetics – or even Duchamp – it's clear that architecture can be considered art – as art can be called architecture. It's not a question of definitions, classifications, media, history, practice, technique, skill, use... it's only a matter of judgement, at least from the point of view of aesthetics. What divided art and architecture – interest and, in particular, use – is no longer an issue, let alone a reason for demoting a presentation from beautiful to merely agreeable. But useful-

179

ness, however insignificant today for differentiating between the products of art and architecture, still haunts the relationship between the two practices. With few exceptions, architecture must be useful and serve the client whereas art can still afford to be useless and capricious, whether the art work includes architecture or not. Art can dig into the history and politics of architecture, exploring complex – and timely – issues that simply cannot be addressed by making a building. Thus, Carsten Höller revives Krutikow's flying city (1928), albeit on a smaller scale. Manfred Pernice's constructions show the traces of several (failed) attempts to install a window, revealing the process of trial and error in architectural planning. Gregor Schneider seems to be doing psychoanalysis with a house, treating every room as if it were an endlessly analysable dream. Michel Majerus covers the Brandenburg Gate in Berlin with a life-size image of a social housing project in the city, fusing high and low architecture. Monica Bonvicini makes a floor that crumbles as soon as you walk on it – adding 'feminine' fragility to the macho durability of the building.

While liberated from use, art suffered from a reduction in forms – dwindling from a panoply of everyday objects to the media of the fine arts – a reduction from which art is still trying to recover. But architecture also suffered from its focus on function, whether expressed through specialization, building codes, law, clients, technology, insurance, planning, money and, above all, time.[11] The different relation to time – art as ephemeral, architecture as durable – is a relic from Kantian aesthetics that has not yet expired. Art still must change – a condition expressed through the ephemeral nature of the art exhibition. By extension, art as architecture can be highly flexible, parasitic, temporary, unplanned, make-shift and, most importantly, untouched by an endless parade of building inspectors. Indeed, art seems to maintain its autonomy by producing architectural works that are mobile. Mobility is a way for contemporary artists to protect their freedom as they build buildings. If a structure can be moved, taken apart or taken off an existing building – even if the structure is large and useful – it can still be seen as a work of art and thus escape rules dictated to permanent structures. Surprisingly, the law respects the original terms of Kantian aesthetics and thus the autonomy of art – a situation best exploited by Atelier van Lieshout. The Rotterdam collective is not only specialized in mobile structures but also tends to operate without permits, precisely because its creations – whether dwellings, alcohol, guns or even explosives – fall into the domain of art.

Architecture, while bogged down by the law, is also not under pressure to change – at least not as rapidly as art, whether one considers the style of the building or its life span. Through the law, architecture is colonized by space and time; like the law itself, it cannot respond so easily to change, whether a political crisis, an evolving historical debate, a wave of refugees, a weekend of ravers or even a community's need for a change in the urban landscape. Given the role of mobility today, the sluggishness of architecture threatens to marginalize the practice with respect to significant social and historical movements, which can be easily captured by art's celerity. The high cost of building has made architecture respond to mobility by catering to an elite instead of other groups of mobiles – Rem Koolhaas's work for Prada contrasts nicely here with MVRDV's unrealized project *Pig City*, 2001, which gives the animals more room and eliminates the need for transporting them. But the most popular projects of the last decade – Frank Gehry's Guggenheim branch in Bilbao and Daniel Libeskind's design for the Jewish Museum in Berlin come to mind – demonstrate that architecture has also responded to mobility with buildings that are more like art. But architecture as art seems too preoccupied with form, exploring a newly-found flexibility in materials and means here, as always, within the confines created by clients, commissions and inspectors. Often, the lessons of Conceptual Art and Relational Aesthetics seem to be missing along with insights offered by artists such as Gordon Matta-Clark or even Gregor Schneider and Manfred Pernice. As a result, the buildings can remain stubbornly autonomous – massive sculptures that have difficulty taking into account the existence of multi-media explorations, temporary interventions or structures that are completed by the chance interventions of users. Even architecture's forays into parasitism – manifest in the building extension – are forced to aim for autonomy. Ultimately, architecture's autonomy tends to be expressed mainly through form and thus cannot be equated with the freedom enjoyed by art – and first established by Kant. Museums for architecture may exist, but, unfortunately, a museum *for buildings* has not yet been built.

Art with Architecture Again

After a long detour, it's possible to grasp the differences between the contemporary fusion between art and architecture and earlier manifestations of this fusion, from Futurism to Constructivism. Contemporary creations, however similar, often turn the terms of their predecessors upside-down, precisely because they use the lessons of Conceptual Art and Relational Aesthetics, from parasitism to incompletion. Today, internationalism has become a way to express locality, individuality and site. Thus, Dominique Gonzalez-Foerster's *Park – Plan d'évasion*, 2002, was not an ideal park made for every city in the world but instead was made of elements taken from parks around the world: a telephone cell from Brazil, a rock from Mexico, a bench from Taiwan, with others. Similarly, Tobias Rehberger's *Casino Dresdner Bank*, 2002, a design for the restaurant of the bank's headquarters in Frankfurt, represents the many foreign offices of the bank through individual tables created according to the artist's interpretation of the cities, from Singapore to New York. Each table includes individual seating, flooring and light fixtures, which dim or lighten according to the local time zone. While lending a particular perspective and locality to the 'non-place' of internationalism, contemporary artists also attempt to individualize the endless series. Manfred Pernice's *Dosentreff '00* (Can meeting '00), 2000, offers a group of wooden canisters, named after people and places. Angela Bulloch's pixel light boxes, however similar, show different scenes in enlarged pixel form, whether a sequence from *Blow Up*, the BBC news or a view of the Pacific rim – the latter appearing sideways on the facade of the Norddeutsche Landesbank in Hanover. Even novelty is rejected with parasitic interventions such as Jorge Pardo's *Eiger, Mönch, Jungfrau*, 2002, which simply added a coat of yellow paint to revive a Swiss highway rest station, originally designed by A. Casoni and D. Casoni in Basel.

What about utopia – the elusive dream that was chased by so many artists, designers and architects at the beginning of the last century?

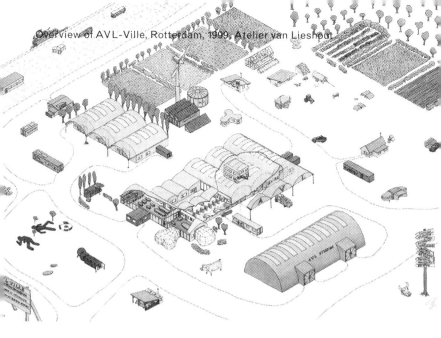

Overview of AVL-Ville, Rotterdam, 1999, Atelier van Lieshout

AVL-Ville transport, 2001. Photo D.J. Wooldrik

AVL-Ville, 2001. Photo D.J. Wooldrik

AVL-Ville flag, 2001. Photo D.J. Wooldrik

Favela, 2001. Photo AVL-Ville

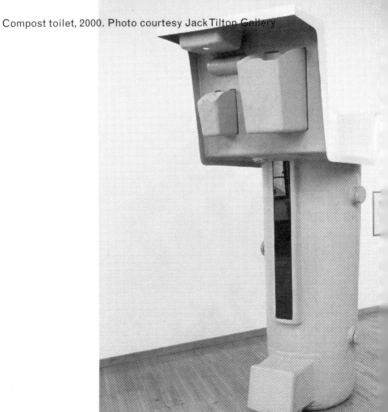

Compost toilet, 2000. Photo courtesy Jack Tilton Gallery

The most critical response comes from Atelier van Lieshout with *AVL-Ville*, 2001–2002. At Atelier van Lieshout's headquarters at the Rotterdam harbour, *AVL-Ville* emerged as a city with the aim of being a free state, complete with housing, farming, education, sewage, public transport, currency and health care along with AVL extras, such as a bomb factory and beds for group sex. From the beginning, AVL-founder Joep van Lieshout has insisted that the project, however expansive, is not utopian.[12] The artist has no interest in utopia, because it simply cannot be realized. *AVL-Ville* did not have to wait decades to be realized as Krutikow's flying city had to wait for Carsten Höller to come along in order to see the light of day. Shifting from utopia to practice, AVL managed to build what most others have left at the planning stage.

But AVL questions the idealism and the ideals of utopian projects on several other counts. Far from creating a brand new world, AVL often deploys materials with a history of other uses, from shipping containers, which are converted into working and living spaces, to scaffolding, which forms the structure for the leisure centre *Sportopia*, 2002. As a Relational work, *AVL-Ville* is meant to be used collectively, but users are not considered to be equal. For living, there is the *Favela House AVL-Ville*, 2001, along with the luxurious *Maxi Capsule Luxus*, 2002, and the more basic *Mini Capsule Side Entrance (6 units)*, 2002 (see elsewhere in this publication). At once mobile and modular, these units do not follow a definitive master plan for ideal urban living but can change according to the evolving users' needs – endlessly expandable in the case of the favela house, and stacked like building blocks in the case of the hotel capsules. Most importantly, *AVL-Ville* is free from the morality that haunts many utopian projects – the biopolitical dimension that Foucault linked to the state's oppressive attempts to organize all aspects of human life, from sexuality to sanitation, from insanity to health.[13] Thus, the AVL constitution allows inhabitants to decide upon their own pleasures – and pains – while the city itself includes facilities for all types of sex along with 'anti-utopian' elements such as the factory for weapons and bombs. While AVL may embrace internation-

185

alism, it's by creating a mobile city – not one city for every place in the world but a city that can move anywhere, anytime. All the structures in *AVL-Ville*, including the compost toilets, have no foundations and thus can be taken apart and moved elsewhere in the space of an afternoon. Like the 'Parasite Paradise' exhibition in Leidsche Rijn near Utrecht itself, *AVL-Ville* is not forever but for now. Of course, it's up to each user to decide just how long now will last.

1 P. Monier, *Histoire des arts qui ont un rapport au dessein* (Paris 1698).
2 Immanuel Kant, '§ 2. Das Wohlgefallen, welches das Geschmacksurtieil bestimmt, ist ohne alles Interesse,' *Kritik der Urteilskraft* (Frankfurt am Main 1974), pp.116 -117. The arguments presented here are all included in the first book, Kant's analytic of the beautiful.
3 Karl Friedrich Schinkel (1823), quoted in Christoph Martin Vogtherr, 'Kunstgenuß versus Kunstwissenschaft. Berliner Museumskonzeptionen bis 1830', *Museumsinszenierungen*, rewritten by A. Joachimides, S. Kuhrau, V. Vahrson & N. Bernau (Dresden, Basel 1995), p. 47. Vogtherr recounts the debate, incited by Alois Hirt, who had his own moderate plan for the museum.
4 See Peter Osborne's introductory essay, *Conceptual Art* (London 2002), pp. 18 -19.
5 Alexander Alberro, 'Reconsidering Conceptual Art, 1966 –1977,' *Conceptual Art: A Critical Anthology* (Cambridge, MA 1999), pp. xvi-xvii.
6 Of course, this interpretation counters Lawrence Weiner, who insists that the declaration of intent brings the work into existence, even if it is never executed. The language and the material referred to are included in the work, but not the site, nor even the lettering.
7 Two major figures of Conceptual Art went on to use architecture: Dan Graham with pavilions and Vito Acconci with public interventions. The move to physical structures from ephemeral forms (distribution in Graham's case and performance in Acconci's case) would merit a separate study.
8 Nicolas Bourriaud, *Esthétique relationnelle* (Dijon 1998). A key exhibition remains *Traffic*, CAPC, Musée d'art contemporain Bordeaux, 1996.
9 Thierry de Duve, *Kant after Duchamp* (Cambridge, MA 1996). See also De Duve, *Au nom de l'art* (Paris 1989).
10 Jens Haaning is a master at exploiting the relative economic autonomy of the museum and gallery. *Foreigners Free*, 1997, 2001, let foreigners into the museum for free – a benefit generally enjoyed by local children, war veterans and the handicapped. *Travel Agency*, 1997, transformed a gallery into an airplane sales ticket office, which sold the tickets with the lower sales tax only granted to art works. At Olso's Kunstnernes Hus, Haaning sold everyday goods from Denmark at a 40% discount, since the goods are not subject to import taxes when brought into Norway as art works. See *Hello, My Name is Jens Haaning* (Dijon 2002).
11 Of course, it's precisely these terms that would make most architects shy away from welcoming art works into their field, whereas aesthetics has become more open.
12 See 'Up the Organization. Jennifer Allen Talks with AVL's Joep van Lieshout,' *Artforum* (April 2001), pp. 104 -111, especially 108.
13 For a discussion of biopolitics, see the final section of Michel Foucault, *La volonté de savoir* (Paris 1976).

The event

'Beyond' organized the open-air exhibition 'Parasite Paradise', held from 1 August to 29 September 2003, and is to realize a number of 'Parasite Spots' in Leidsche Rijn in the years to come.

'Beyond' (www.beyondutrecht.nl) is the long-term arts project for the Utrecht Vinex site of Leidsche Rijn. 'Beyond' realizes temporary projects and permanent artworks divided into six programmes: Action Research, Parasites, Looping, Direction Artists, Artists' Residencies and White Spots. 'Beyond' projects stitch together the architecture, landscape architecture and urban development of Leidsche Rijn.

'Beyond' is an initiative of the City of Utrecht in collaboration with SKOR (Foundation for Art and Public Space) and with funding by the Ministry of Spatial Planning, Housing and the Environment (VROM/IPSV), K.F. Hein Fonds and Elise Mathilde Fonds. With thanks to Walter Lenting, Nico Jansen and Wouter van der Poel. www.beyondutrecht.nl

Project manager of 'Parasite Paradise' and 'Parasite Spots': Tom van Gestel in cooperation with Monique Dirven (Explorama), Mariette Dölle (City of Utrecht), Trudie Timmerman, Wendel ten Arve and Hanneke Janssens (SKOR).